TOWARD A RECOVERY OF CHRISTIAN BELIEF

TOWARD A RECOVERY OF CHRISTIAN BELIEF

The Rutherford Lectures

Carl F. H. Henry

CROSSWAY BOOKS•WHEATON, ILLINOIS
A DIVISION OF GOOD NEWS PUBLISHERS

Toward a Recovery of Christian Belief.

Copyright © 1990 by Carl F. H. Henry.

Published by Crossway Books, a division of
Good News Publishers, Wheaton, Illinois 60187.

Cover illumination: Charles Carruth

First printing, 1990

Printed in the United States of America

Library of Congress Cataloging-in-Publication Data

Henry, Carl Ferdinand Howard, 1913-
    Toward a recovery of Christian belief : The Rutherford lectures,
October 1989 / Carl F.H. Henry.
        p.   cm.
    Includes bibliographical references and index.
    ISBN 0-89107-588-7 :
    1. Apologetics--20th century. 2. Skepticism. 3. Philosophy,
Modern. 4. Evangelicalism. 5. Revelation. 6. Theism.
7. Knowledge, Theory of (Religion) I. Title. II. Title:
Rutherford lectures.
BT1211.H46   1990
201--dc20

                                                          90-80629
                                                          CIP

CONTENTS

FOREWORD

Rutherford House is a center for evangelical publishing and research in Edinburgh, Scotland. Every year we invite a distinguished evangelical leader from outside Scotland to spend a week with us. Previous Rutherford Lecturers have included Professor James I. Packer, Professor Edmund P. Clowney, and Professor Donald A. Carson. We had hoped for a number of years that Dr. Carl F. H. Henry would be able to join us, and I was delighted when he accepted our invitation for 1989 and journeyed to Scotland to deliver the lectures on which this important book is based. From his position at the center of the evangelical world for more than half a century, he is more able than anyone to call us *Toward a Recovery of Christian Belief*, and to do so with passion and intellect alike undiminished by the passage of the years—and in a constantly changing world, in which the recovery rather than the mere defense of the faith is now the issue.

Dr. Henry's rigorous program carried him well outside Scotland. His demanding itinerary took him first to London Theological Seminary and then to the Evangelical Theological College of Wales at Cardiff. After a radio interview on BBC Wales, he delivered the annual Lecture in Contemporary Christianity sponsored by the Evangelical Movement of Wales. Then, in Edinburgh, Scotland, after preaching at Holyrood Abbey Church, he went to New College in the University of Edinburgh to address a seminar, and on to Rutherford House to deliver the Rutherford Lectures. Dr. Henry then travelled to Glasgow, where he lectured to the student body of the Bible Training Institute, and to the divinity faculty of Glasgow University, later addressing a large meeting at St. George's-Tron Church. In Aberdeen there followed an address at Gilcomston South Church and a lecture to students in the faculty of divinity, King's College, University of Aberdeen. The visit concluded with a conference of the Rutherford House Fellowship and other engagements at Tyndale House, Cambridge, as well as a final day of preaching in Eden Baptist Church, Cambridge.

That breathless paragraph sets out the bones of a breathless ten-day visit. In the chapters that follow, we have an opportunity to reflect at more leisure on the message Dr. Henry brought to the United Kingdom and now sets forth for the Church at large, exploiting to the full his remarkable gift for shedding light on the clouded contemporary scene and enabling us to gain afresh the bearings of faith.

Nigel M. de S. Cameron, Warden
Rutherford House
Edinburgh, Scotland

INTRODUCTION

To present the 1989 Rutherford Lectures in Scotland was a high privilege. The return to Edinburgh, always a favorite city, renewed memorable hours with professors at both New College and Free Church College.

In this volume I address issues that to me seem highly important for evangelical Christianity in the last decade of the twentieth century and beyond. Their conceptual interrelationships are apparent.

The first lecture observes that unless the Christian world- and life-view is championed as a comprehensive totality, its intellectual power is soon lost. Ever since apostolic times, Christian postulates have repeatedly been diluted and diminished by scholars who, under the influence of speculative theories, venture to retain Christian principles only piecemeal. This process has led to a gradual and continuing sacrifice of basic Christian doctrines, until neopaganism now routinely leaves its mark upon the influential secular centers of Western learning.

The second lecture concerns theological method. It commends deductive theology over inductive, indicating its special importance for a century in which empiricism and existentialism have penetrated deeply into evangelical ranks. It discusses the inescapable role of presuppositions and faces the issue of distinguishing valid and invalid assumptions. It stresses rational consistency as a test of truth, lest presuppositional theology veer into fideism. It identifies the Biblical canon, moreover, as the Christian verifying principle. It emphasizes that while belief is not antecedently necessary to comprehend Christian truths, personal appropriation of these truths is indispensable for participating in the benefits of redemption. It refuses to settle for mere theological probability. Amid the quest for certainty, however, it emphasizes that God's Spirit uses truth as a means of persuasion and confers personal assurance as a divine gift.

The third lecture concentrates more fully on the distinctive axioms that underlie Christianity's core beliefs and identifies logical consistency as a negative test of truth. Indicating the inevitable difficulties of a merely empirical theology, the lecture notes that even professing empiricists harbor unacknowledged presuppositions. It applauds the view of the Protestant Reformers that belief in the existence of God, of the world, and of other selves is pre-philosophical.

The original final lecture dealt with the recent recovery of canonical theology by Professor Brevard Childs and other scholars who reject higher criticism's century-old effort to locate earlier and more reliable sources behind the Scriptures, sources that the Biblical writers then supposedly mythologized in order to promote the Hebrew cult. While I welcome any movement toward canonical theology as the Christian verifying principle, I disavow Dr. Childs's unnecessary critical concessions in that they weaken the objective truth and historical factuality of Scriptural teaching. Because of the length of this discussion, however, this particular lecture will appear separately in an early issue of the *Scottish Bulletin of Evangelical Theology* published by Rutherford House.

The brief final chapter here contains added reflections on the theme of my lectures and notes its special significance for the present evangelical scene. The fact is that since mid-century no feature of American theology has been as prominent as the return of serious systematic theology by evangelical writers. This development is all the more welcome because recent emphasis on experiential religion has tended to thrust into the background the importance of doctrinal controls. It is a propitious sign indeed that both evangelical students and the laity generally sense the need and importance of greater theological depth. Without clear and credible doctrinal directives, Christian experience fades in conviction, even as doctrinal assent devoid of personal appropriation spells spiritual impoverishment.

During my visit to Britain, where these lectures were delivered in October 1989 at Rutherford House in Edinburgh, one or another of them was given also to the divinity faculties of Aberdeen and Glasgow universities, as well as at Tyndale House, Cambridge, England, and to members of the Evangelical Movement of Wales, in Cardiff. Additional addresses were given at London

Theological Seminary, founded by Dr. D. Martyn Lloyd-Jones, at the Bible Training Institute of Glasgow, and at the Evangelical Theological College of Wales. The first and third lectures were presented *extempore* at Southeastern Baptist Theological Seminary in Wake Forest, North Carolina; the third lecture was similarly given at the University of Virginia under sponsorship of the Christian Studies Center.

For these and other arrangements, as well as for gracious hospitality, I express appreciation to the Rev. Dr. N. M. de S. Cameron, warden of Rutherford House.

Carl F. H. Henry

ONE

Living at the Bottom of a Well

Not long ago I traveled to Purdue University to address an informal faculty luncheon arranged by a dozen or so evangelical believers among them; as it turned out, about one hundred professors attended.

Earlier that morning I had flown from Washington, D.C., to Dayton, Ohio, where I then caught a regional commuter plane to Indianapolis. There I was met by a Purdue professor, an engineering specialist, who in a four-seater Cessna piloted me and his pastor, a former student of mine, on the last leg of the trip to the Lafayette campus. We had scarcely reached 4,000 feet aloft when the professor-pilot laconically remarked that the plane spotter had just died.

Not being any more comfortable than I was about an apparently unexpected death almost a mile in the sky, my clergyman friend asked, "What does that mean?" "No problem," answered the professor-pilot. "It just means that no one can now tell where we are."

That succinct exchange, it seems to me, in some ways aptly describes our current condition. The West has lost its moral and epistemic compass bearings. It has no shared criterion for judging whether human beings are moving up or down, standing still, or merely on the move only God knows where.

For many centuries the Western world recognized an absolute norm, namely, the will of the self-revealed God published in divinely inspired Scripture. The Bible could tell us "where we are," "from where we have come," and "where we are going." Thanks to its Scriptural commitments, the West towered head and shoulders above its pagan past.

But now the prospect of neo-paganism confronts us everywhere. No longer are radical pagans scaling the walls of modern life only here and there; they have entered the cultural mainstream, are dancing in the streets, and are even setting a comprehensive agenda for the future.

To anyone familiar with the history of ideas it is obvious that the unique features of the Western view of life and of the cosmos are largely rooted in the Hebrew-Christian Scriptures and, beyond that, in the supernatural God of the Bible. Severed from those roots, these distinctives have no real prospect of survival. A recent reminder of this essential connection comes even from the agnostic social critic Allan Bloom in *The Closing of the American Mind*.[1] The Bible, he says, provided our model for a comprehensive vision of the cosmic order. But the contemporary forfeiture of the public significance of Scripture has negated the necessity and possibility of the Biblical world-explanation. The search for an alternative model is beset with confusion, and Western society drifts indecisively toward chaos. Secular scholars seem unable to tell us where we are.

"They lived at the bottom of a well," reads a fascinating line from Lewis Carroll's *Alice in Wonderland*. I venture to suggest that in terms of the history of ideas the "they" may well be "we" ourselves; for our beleaguered generation, the well has run dry. Once it was refreshingly brimful; once it nurtured the life of a spiritual and moral society unmatched in the history of mankind. Hebrew theism, writes Eric Voegelin, precipitated "a break in the pattern of civilizational courses," "a new genus of society"; in fact, the ancient nation of Israel began at a level at which other respectable societies "have difficulty even ending."[2] But now we cower at the bottom of a well run dry, one that offers little prospect but stagnation and decay.

I propose to survey the West's costly stifling of God after Jesus Christ came into the world and the early Church launched the Christian era and put Graeco-Roman paganism on the defensive. The subsequent suffocation of God betrayed Western thought finally to neo-paganism—to a raw naturalism that so suffocates every last vestige of transcendence that it almost borders on ancient pre-Christian motifs of chance and fatalistic determinism. Even the paganism of New Testament times had more in common with Christianity, said C.S. Lewis in his inaugural lecture at Cambridge University, than ancient paganism has with the crass neo-paganism emerging in our own day.

The younger generation today scarcely realizes the staggering debt that Western thought owes to the Biblical heritage or how far modern culture has drifted from the Scriptural foundations, even if many parents and grandparents still cling to broken fragments of that inheritance. To the Judeo-Christian view we owe the beliefs that:

- The universe is a purposive divine creation;
- All human life is sacred, and human beings are of equal dignity;

- History is linear and moves toward a final goal;
- Nature is an orderly system, and man is its responsible steward;
- Righteousness will triumph in a final decisive conquest of evil;
- Our earthly life does not exhaust human existence but looks ahead to the resurrection of the dead and to a final, comprehensive judgment of humanity and the nations.

Many authorities—both secular and Christian—concede and underscore these claims and much more. One thinks at once of the historian F. A. Foakes-Jackson, who tracks all humanitarian movements of the West to their origin in the theology of the Cross; of the political scientist John Hallowell, who affirms that the loss of the Biblical doctrine of man's creation in the *imago Dei* leaves us today without any firm case for human equality; of Alfred North Whitehead and Stanley Jaki, who declare that pursuit of the detailed behavior of nature by modern science was nurtured by the Christian view of God as orderly Creator and sovereign Preserver of the cosmos; of Ernst Bloch and Johannes Metz, who trace the modern revolutionary longing for a political utopia to the Biblical emphasis on a future final kingdom of justice, even if (let me add) liberation theology gives this hope a reactionary form.

To be sure, it is not only in recent modern times, or only first in the Middle Ages, that Christianity has had to contend with the dilution of its message. Not only by its foes but also by some of its professing friends the core content of Christianity has frequently been clouded. Early Christians coped with spiritual delinquents and deformers, as well as with others the likes of ourselves, as Paul's letters to the Corinthians remind us. For their earlier disobedience, the ancient Hebrews were sent into Babylonian exile.

But such defection did not in the past and does not in the present invalidate Hebrew-Christian monotheism and the Biblical revelation. The Bible is not disproved, and Biblical theism is not undermined, by the dalliances even of American televangelists. Scripture declares unapologetically and insistently that Jesus Christ alone is sinless and that all mere humans are sinners; popular televangelists are clearly not exceptions to the rule. But Scripture also warns that the deliberate defamation of the Christian witness by those of us who should be role models is no light offense.

Even before the Middle Ages Christianity was politicized and Biblical revelation was put at risk through an elevation of church authority. The Protestant Reformers protested against:

- The medieval addition of legends and myths to Biblical Christianity;
- The distortion of justification by a "faith-plus-works" misunderstanding that embraced sacramental salvation;
- The contraction of the role of divine revelation and of the noetic and volitional consequences of sin, and the promotion, instead, of natural theology and empirical "proof" of God's existence.

From its beginnings in 1600 with the Jesuit philosopher Descartes, modern philosophy substituted speculative theism for revelatory Biblical theism. It divorced the case for God's existence from special divine revelation, from God's singular Incarnation in Jesus Christ, and from inspired prophetic-apostolic teaching. Instead, modern philosophy relied on philosophical argumentation from the not-God, that is, from nature, or from the pattern of history, or from mankind—especially from human mind and conscience.

To be sure, early modern philosophy retained many notable features of the Biblically revealed view of God. It spoke of God as the almighty Father and as infinite personality, in contrast to Greek philosophers for whom personality somehow restricts infinity and who therefore regarded personality and infinity as incompatible alternatives. Early modern philosophical theists, moreover, tended to speak of God as both supernatural mind and active will instead of viewing the supernatural mainly in terms of eternal ideas or forms.

Like the pre-Christian Greek classical thinkers, modern philosophers broadly emphasized the priority of the spiritual world, the essential uniqueness of man, and the objective character of truth and the good. Nonetheless, modern theists and idealists—Descartes, Leibniz, Hegel, and others—produced highly conflicting views of God; the supernatural phantom became increasingly difficult to define.

Still, in contrast to the Greeks on whom they leaned more and more, early modern thinkers unwittingly preserved certain Biblical emphases peculiar to the Judeo-Christian revelation:

- Matter was no longer viewed as eternal but as somehow created (although creation was sometimes conceived in terms of emanation or evolution);
- Matter and the body were no longer considered evil. The Platonic view of an evil body gave way to the Pauline doctrine of "the flesh," which presupposed a divinely gifted body and soul that, due to a voluntary human fall into sin, is now in the service of unregenerate dispositions;
- The golden age of history was no longer associated only with human beginnings but was located also in the future as a final, consummatory kingdom of righteousness.

For all that, because these early modern philosophers distanced themselves from the self-revealing God of the Bible, they could not resist making further concessions to naturalism. Slowly but surely, despite its early theistic intentions, modern philosophy came to affirm:

- Nature alone is the ultimate reality;
- Man is essentially a complex animal;
- Truth and the good are relative and changing.

Assuredly, at first only a nineteenth-century elite mounted this platform; these views had not yet become, as in the recent past, the covert conceptuality that underlies liberal arts learning.

But despite its accelerating revolt against the Christian outlook, even this nineteenth-century naturalism, like the speculative theism that it had disowned, also retained, unawares, certain elements of the Biblical view:

- Nature, which it declared to be the ultimate reality, it identified as intrinsically *rational*, that is, as a logically ordered system;
- The human species it regarded as the climax and summit of the world of nature and as distinctively able to discern the inherent rationale of cosmic reality;
- Truth and the good, although changing, it nonetheless considered relatively durable.

So deeply had the Biblical view penetrated Western thought that both modern idealism and its rebellious counterpart, naturalism, despite their disavowal of the Christian heritage, clung to significant elements of orthodox theism, albeit in a seriously compromised way.

Early in the twentieth century, naturalism divested itself more thoroughly of these surviving Biblical influences. Scientists spoke less about the objective rationality of nature and more about creative models through which the observer represents both nature and history. Existential theory located the distinctiveness of mankind in the human capacity for decision rather than in a conceptual capacity for discerning an objective pattern in nature. Once the living God is banished, both Jesus Christ and the Bible become cognitive orphans. Not only are history and nature rendered godless, so that they can be assimilated readily either to mechanical determinism or to chaos, and not only is mankind rendered godless, so that humanity is free to play deity or to consider itself mere soulless specks of cosmic dust, but also the most basic referents of Christianity become embarrassing enigmas. The Bible is declared a dissonant book lacking any cohesive center, elusive in its complexity and bearing an ambiguous witness; its textuality is coordinated with such a plurality of meanings that its revelatory character is emptied into the category of general literature. A century now dawns in which, as G. R. Beasley-Murray puts it, there prevails for the first time an acute "uncertainty as to who Jesus was" and even of what Jesus thought of Himself and His mission.[3]

By the mid-twentieth century, secular humanism, which repudiated all revealed truths and divine commandments, had become the molding metaphysics of Western liberal arts learning. It emphasized that:

- All reality is reducible to impersonal processes and energy events;
- All life, including human life, is transient, and its final destiny is death;
- Truth and the good are culture-conditioned distinctions that the human race projects upon the cosmos and history.

The implication is clear: humanity's coming of age requires rejecting all transcendentally fixed and final authority.

At the same time, even secular humanism was unable

to divorce itself completely from the Biblical heritage. Into its naturalistic control beliefs it injected an agenda of social concerns involving universal justice, human rights, ecological matters, and compassion for the poor and weak. But thus to commend an agenda of fixed social imperatives clearly counters humanism's basic assumption that moral principles are culturally relative and inconstant. As conservative critics like D. Elton Trueblood pointed out, humanist social concerns did not stem from their naturalistic worldview, but rather were borrowed from the Judeo-Christian heritage by a metaphysics reluctant to acknowledge its indebtedness. Simultaneously, the more radical naturalists conceded that their emphasis—namely, that reality reduces to impersonal and impermanent natural elements and forces—cannot accommodate changeless moral absolutes. On one occasion when President Frank Rhodes of Cornell University told a Harvard audience that campuses need to assume at least some responsibility for the intellectual and moral well-being of students, he was faced by critical hearers demanding to know just whose morality would or should be taught.

Today's debate focuses on the propriety or impropriety of a role for transcendence in a universe conceived only in terms of impersonal processes and quantum events. The so-called radically secular Christian-Marxist debate, the contemporary drug culture, and the rise of deconstructionist philosophy all reflect, in three different ways, the current struggle over vanishing vestiges of Biblical teaching.

In the secular dialogue between so-called Christian radicals and Marxists, both sides reject the supernatural and adhere to a naturalistic worldview. The center of the debate is the traditional Marxist affirmation of economic determinism and the inevitable historical triumph of the proletariat. The ongoing nonfulfillment of Communist promises and expectations of utopia has promoted skepticism about determinism and inevitability.

"Secular Christian" radicals insist on a factor of personal transcendence and on the importance of human action and praxis in order to consummate the Communist revolution. Unlike many Greek philosophers and Spinoza and Hegel, who consider the world to be a self-sufficient reality, these radicals nonetheless support the Christian emphasis that the universe is not sealed against the possibility of transformation and of a new creation. Man's destiny is linked, they say, to human decision and action, even if so-called Christian-Marxist debate is waged perversely in the context of a one-layer theory of reality, a naturalistic ontology that excludes a supernatural God. Yet in discussing man the "secular Christians" invoke categories beyond those of physics and biology, psychology and sociology. But at the fringes, where naturalism becomes mystical and ambiguous, they forfeit the very theistic realities that illumine the finite. By excluding supernatural presence and purpose in nature and history they cannot convincingly resist the ancient notion that human history is a great cycle where reality, as an eternal self-sustaining mechanism, not only lacks fixed meaning but also, after a series of predetermined events, returns at last to its primal state.

The countercultural drug surge represents an even more conspicuous effort to thrust human selfhood into transcendence. Rejecting technological scientism as the key to the meaning of life, it instead seeks personal significance through an inner consciousness-exploding experience. Skirting the ramparts of scientific empiricism, it promotes what it considers an "out-of-body" recreational sacrament of an intensely personal, quasi-religious happening of an anti-materialist kind. Some addicts have described the experience in terms of being internally reborn. The estimated number of Americans who have illegally used drugs both casually and addictively is about 60 million; some observers believe that some 40 million continue to be involved, over a million being addicted to cocaine or crack.

Evangelical Christians in the United States who claim to be spiritually "born again" are now also thought to number over 60 million. Long before the recent countercultural movement, evangelicals emphasized that mankind's everyday conscious experience is in some respects abnormal; that humanity's present selfhood is skewed and requires a new kind of living; and that no gratifying alternative exists apart from a vital link to the transcendent realm through a dynamic internal experience of spiritual regeneration.

Emphasis on spiritual new birth and eternal life is an essential element in Jesus' teaching and in the New Testament writings. But modern experience-centered denominations, most notably the Pentecostal movement, tend to isolate this emphasis from a credally oriented heritage and are theologically less precise than the historic mainline churches. Although Pentecostalism is, to be sure, far removed from any pursuit of a "better life" through chemistry, certain aspects of Pentecostalism are notably similar to psychedelic phenomena insofar as emphasis falls on an intense personal experience independent of a credally oriented community and occurring in a theologically imprecise context. Pentecostalism's experiential features, moreover, are held to shatter universal linguistic and conceptual limits.

But a striking difference distances Pentecostal experience from the "quasi-religious" events of the drug culture; from the current deconstructionist movement in philosophy, which deliberately rejects metaphysical theism and all *logos*-structured existence; and from so-called secular Christian Marxists who abandon the supernatural. Although Pentecostalism lacks a systematic theology and its beliefs are not credally structured, it insists nonetheless on the objective existence of the triune God, the Lordship of Jesus Christ the God-man, the personal reality of the Holy Spirit, and the authority of the Bible. In short, Pentecostalism's offer of an alternative mode of living champions an experiential religious counterclaim to the secular drug culture. Deconstructionism, meanwhile, in its rejection of *logos* and rationality and of an objectively existing God, extends ontologically, as it were, specific extrarational implications of the psychedelic phenomenon.

In contrast to the credal precision of historic Christian supernaturalism, psychedelic exploration involves a cognitively amorphous relationship to the transcendent; it yields a drug-induced mysticism in which self-transcendence is not assuredly in touch with a reality beyond one's own selfhood. The supposedly higher world in which the self is immersed is characterless and indefinable; it is transrational or superrational, outside the realm of propositional formulation. What constitutes the experient's self-fulfillment is as obscure as what constitutes self-transcendence. We therefore face diametrically opposed approaches to transcendence: either conscious-expanding psychedelic experience or divine propositional revelation.

Much as some practitioners portray indulgence in hallucinatory drugs as a kind of religious experience, it in fact warps the human psyche and disregards the image of God in which human beings are created. The experience is detached not only from rational criteria, but also from moral concerns by the relaxing of long-revered universal ethical imperatives. It manifests no intelligibly grounded response to the Transcendent and is empty of publicly shareable meaning, virtue, and duty. Chemically induced ecstasy is a return to magic; vibrations replace syllogisms and pharmacology replaces theology as its context. To say that psychedelic experience is akin to a spiritual sacrament merely enlarges the contemporary ambiguity concerning the definition of religion and of religious experience.

The current exaggeration of an internal experience into life's ultimate dimension is not unrelated to present-day theological and cultural illiteracy. Where it impacts upon the drug culture, sub-theological Christianity offers mainly a counterexperience too elemental to register deep societal consequences. There is the further risk that a generation of converted acidheads may consider their turning to Christianity but an exchange of one set of feelings for another. All too many Americans already believe, as Russell

Hittinger notes, "that a satisfying religious experience can be had without worrying about propositional truths."[4] This widening contrast between private spiritual experience and publicly shareable truth, even to the point of ambiguity concerning a transcendent religious object, together with an emphasis on personal creativity in respect to the mystical metaphysical, has far-reaching implications. Mediated revelational knowledge is devalued; moreover, the term *revelation* is exploited if, by merely ingesting some particular chemical compound, one searches for immediate internal relationships with the ultimate world and for something directly felt and mystically divine. Such procedure is not unlike striving to plunge oneself into a new and different world by switching to erotic television channels in quest of psychic orgasm. In the absence of fixed epistemic and ethical controls, a light-headed, drug-dependent generation is doomed to rudderless existence. Loosed from rationality and morality, its so-called religious experience soon collapses into the subrational and subethical. The submergence of God in ineffable data is a first step toward putting Deity out to die. Once God is pushed to the brink of language, Christianity will be criticized, and not surprisingly, for trying to define Him.[5] What is here at stake is not only individual worth and meaning and the purpose of the universe, but also any understanding of the existence of God the transcendent Creator and Preserver of life as well as of mankind's own nature and destiny.

By deliberately repudiating the last traces of transcendence framed even in sub-Christian terms, deconstructionist philosophers plummet us to the bottom of the theological well. Whereas psychedelic experience probes the prospect of a transcendent superrational reality, one that devalues universal cognitive and ethical categories, and whereas the radical Christian-Marxist dialogue assumes a one-level ontology and, within it, probes possibilities of historical transcendence beyond cosmic determinism, post-theistic atheism, or deconstructionism, tries to overturn the whole history of Western thought by turning it loose from God and logic, from verificatory criteria and shared verbal signification. Deconstructionism disowns any remnant of transcendence that derives genetically and logically from the Judeo-Christian heritage. In calling for a post-metaphysical age it champions the end of both theism and metaphysics. Deconstructionists would expunge from Western thought any emphasis on an objectively existing deity. One commentator portrays the movement as the "dance of death upon the tomb of God."

Post-theistic atheism no doubt has a legitimate complaint against the long succession of conflicting and competing conceptions of deity that crowd Western thought from the time of Plato to that of today's process philosophers. Put forward as alternatives to the self-revealing God of the Bible, this panorama of conjectural gods has long posed a discouraging identity crisis. It is not surprising, therefore, that twentieth-century philosophy closes the second Christian millennium in a climactic admission that the durable alternative is not the God of Plato, of Aristotle, of the Stoics, of Descartes, of Leibniz, of Kant, of Hegel, of Whitehead, or of a hundred others.

While philosophical deconstructionists join in trying

to put these ailing divinities out of their misery, they are at the same time specially hostile toward the revelatory Judeo-Christian view, considering it past recall or recovery. Their intense animosity toward Biblical theism, however, unwittingly acknowledges Christian orthodoxy's incomparable hold on the masses.

The deconstructionist discounting of Christianity is ventured in the interest of a philosophical reconstruction that stresses the human knower's creative[6] contribution to the content of knowledge and that proposes a return to the ancient Greek cosmic philosophers for a fresh beginning in the history of ideas. Marxists applaud this deconstruction of Western philosophy in order to promote their own Socialist theory that links contemporary naturalism with pre-Christian and pre-Socratic materialism and degrades theism as myth.

For this colossal inversion modern scholars have themselves to blame. Ongoing dilution of the essentials of Biblical theism, through concessions to one and then another neoteric speculative theory, seriously impaired Judeo-Christian core beliefs. University scholars eagerly truncated the living God of the Bible, sundering Him from nature and history and paying only grudging, temporary tribute to this or that surviving morsel of the West's Christian inheritance. Repeated deference to novelties, to which Scriptural concepts were routinely adjusted, finally forfeited cognitive initiative to contemporary conjectural alternatives to the Biblical view.

During the first half of the twentieth century, anti-intellectualism inundated professedly Christian theology, most notably in the religious views of Rudolf Bultmann and the early Karl Barth. Although Barth finally rejected Bultmann's existential reduction of Christian beliefs, deconstructionists welcome Barth's elevation of the actuality of God above the logical law of contradiction; they see it as an unwitting contribution to their claim that an objectively existing God is but a byproduct of human imagination.

Particularly in the secular universities of the West little attention was paid to intermediating religious views. The half-gods of one generation soon become the laughingstock of the next. The dwarfed *Logos* has yielded to secular humanism as the masked metaphysics of modernity. Now the tide is shifting to naked paganism. The term *god* is stripped of metaphysical significance; no objective criteria are acknowledged for telling right from wrong or truth from error. At the bottom of the well the last glimmers of light are lowering.

Yet even modernity's intellectually inventive knowers, obsessed with the myth of their unlimited creativity, hesitate to view themselves as mere quantum events and as cogs in a network of impersonal processes. Conscience continues to hail its subjects before a transcendent reality and nurtures an uneasy suspicion that at the end of our philosophical tether the Hound of Heaven whom we have disowned may instead have cornered us at the very bottom of the well. An unseen Presence sporadically breaks the silences; a disconcertingly recognizable voice asks the same discomfiting question that first sounded in Eden after the Fall: "Adam, where are you?" Someone seems after all to know where we are. Through the acrid depths of our crumbling culture echoes a plaint once heard by Jeremiah: "My people have . . . forsaken me, the spring of living water, and have dug their own cisterns, broken cisterns that cannot hold water" (Jeremiah 2:13).

TWO

Presuppositions and Theological Method

Empiricism has been much the vogue in recent evangelical theology. While it is not pressed the length of making sensory observation and laboratory verification the only reliable way of knowing, it nonetheless encourages a theological appeal to particulars in search of a universal, rather than postulating a universal explanatory principle subject to testing. Any deductive exposition of Christianity is therefore disparaged.

Modern loss of interest in the history of doctrine plays a part in such discrediting of deductive theology. Many evangelical seminaries in fact offer no course whatever in historical theology. Most conservative Christians are therefore unaware that Christendom's earliest systematic theology began with God as the basic axiom and from this explanatory principle derived the content of the Christian religion. It was Origen (A.D. 250) who, in his *peri archon* (Latin tr., *De principiis*), expounded the implications of divine intelligence and simplicity over against Neo-Platonism's projection of radical transcendence and who deduced theological knowledge of creation and salvation.

Ever since the beginning of the Christian era the operative methodology for systematic theology has been mainly deductive. Augustine and Anselm championed theological deduction. Not until Thomas Aquinas proposed an empirical alternative in the twelfth century was the deductive method seriously disputed; in some respects it prevailed even into the nineteenth century, when Schleiermacher decisively challenged it. The Protestant Reformers employed deduction, although evidentialists currently render this problematical by blending the Reformers' emphasis on general revelation into an empirical approach.

In contrast to their forefathers' affirmation of deduction, evidentialists champion induction; that is, they proceed from nature and man as effects to the existence of an intelligible and moral First Cause of the universe. The so-called proofs or evidences are declared logical struts that promote and support theism.

Theologians who begin a priori with God as their axiom or comprehensive explanatory principle from which they derive all else are derided by evidentialists as being presuppositionalists who merely toy with mental preconceptions. Evidentialists belittle presuppositionalists as sheer fideists who appeal to faith alone and deliberately disengage themselves from and disparage reason and evidence, and who assume in advance what any responsible academician would feel obliged to "prove." Fideists merely announce a conclusion—so the complaint goes—without first arriving at it rationally, and moreover, they deliberately reject any subsequent need for any objective rational test.

It is easy, but nonetheless intellectually irresponsible, to dismiss all evangelical presuppositionalists as mere fideists. Some may fit the complaint, but any sweeping charge merely nurtures a secular misjudgment that detaches faith from reason and links it with presumption. Once this misconception is established, any thinking person would balk at faith; in its place, sophisticated intellectuals would prefer reason as a welcome antidote.

The notion that truth in religion ultimately rests "on faith rather than reasoning or evidence" the philosopher Richard H. Poplin imputes to the apostle Paul.[1] Paul does indeed reject philosophical reasoning or world-wisdom as the Christian way of knowing and, moreover—unlike evidentialists—does not affirm the existence of God on empirical grounds. What Poplin fails to note, however, is that Paul's appeal to faith in no way repudiates either public reason or logic.

More properly labeled as fideists are Søren Kierkegaard and certain Neo-orthodox theologians who dismiss public reason and rational tests as irrelevant to religious truth claims. In affirming the Bible rather than the Koran or the Gita or *Das Kapital* as his starting point, Karl Barth, as Peter Berger protests, at the same time rejects the significance of universal reason as an external test of truth.[2] Barth's early writings—if not his latest also—lend credence to Berger's complaint.

Such views are not to be confused, however, with evangelical orthodoxy. Evangelical theists consider unacceptable any irrationalist claim that intellectual absurdity renders religious beliefs worthy or that spiritual obedience demands a "leap of faith" indifferent to rational considerations.

To disparage some evangelical theists as fideists, moreover, simply because they reject the validity of the standard empirical proofs for God's existence, is patently unjustified. Such disparagement, I contend, inexcusably disengages Biblical theism from the soundest case that evangelical orthodoxy can mount.

My premise is the legitimacy of deductive theology and the invalidity of the evidentialist alternative. The so-called theistic proofs, I maintain, provide no conclusive demonstration of the existence of the self-revealing God of the Bible. To speak more modestly of "evidences" instead of "proofs" requires a fallback to probabilities. If evidentialist argument "establishes" the probability of any divine reality, it romances an un-Scriptural deity more than it reinforces Biblical theism.

Evidentialists who disparage the primacy of faith do evangelical theology no special service. To affirm the priority of faith need not mean, as evidentialists routinely charge, that all presuppositionalists adhere to faith alone *apart from, instead of, or contrary to* reason. To maintain that faith precedes speculative reasoning in establishing certain basic truths does not at all require a dismissal of reason and evidence as irrelevant to authentic faith.

One must contrast the Augustinian formula *credo ut intellegam* ("I believe in order to understand") not only with Thomas Aquinas's formula ("I understand in order to believe"), but equally much with the so-called Tertullian formula *credo quia absurdum* ("I believe what is absurd"). The modern Neo-orthodox revival of Tertullian's slogan was not unrelated to existentialist insistence on the ultimate absurdity of the world, a notion that is neither Biblical nor evangelical.

Evangelical presuppositionalists—as evangelical empiricists or evidentialists now often pejoratively label them—disavow the official Roman Catholic view formulated by Thomas Aquinas and approved by the Council of Trent. The Thomistic view maintains that the existence of God and the existence and immortality of the soul are to be established by empirical evidence and unaided reason, not by the primacy of revelation or faith.

In opposing presuppositionalism, evangelical empiricists lean heavily on Thomas's "five-fold proof." They quite ignore the fact that Thomas himself adopts a presuppositional or deductive approach in regard to such admittedly revealed doctrines as the Trinity and bodily resurrection:

> As the other sciences do not argue in proof of their principles, but argue from their principles to demonstrate other truths in these sciences, so this doctrine does not argue in proof of its principles, which are the articles of faith, but from them it goes on to prove something else; as the Apostle argues from the resurrection of Christ in proof of the general resurrection (I Cor. xv, 12). However, it is to be borne in mind, in regard to the philosophical sciences, that the inferior sciences neither prove their principles nor dispute with those who deny them, but leave this to a higher science; whereas the highest of them, viz., metaphysics, can dispute with one who denies its principles, if only the opponent will make some concession; but if he concedes nothing, it can

TOWARD A RECOVERY OF CHRISTIAN BELIEF

have no dispute with him, though it can answer his arguments. Hence Sacred Scripture, since it has no science above itself, disputes argumentatively with one who denies its principles only if the opponent admits some at least of the truths obtained through divine revelation. Thus, we can argue with heretics from texts in Holy Scripture, and against those who deny one article of faith we can argue from another. If our opponent believes nothing of our divine revelation, there is no longer any means of proving the articles of faith by argument, but only of answering his objections if he has any against faith. Since faith rests upon infallible truth, and since the contrary of a truth can never be demonstrated, it is clear that the proofs brought against faith are not demonstrations, but arguments that can be answered. ("Nature of Sacred Doctrine," *Summa Theologica*, Eighth Article, "Whether Sacred Doctrine is Argumentative?")

If *presuppositionalism* implies that anyone who thinks has presuppositions, then I am unapologetically an evangelical presuppositionalist. In fact, even an empiricist or evidentialist who professes to be wholly free of presuppositions harbors them, however covertly or unwittingly.

I find fideism, moreover, no more inviting or consoling than empiricism. Evangelical Christianity has as little to gain from a theory that—disavowing public reason and logical criteria (including the law of contradiction)—simply takes God for granted, as it does from a view that presumes to derive God from the not-God (whatever aspects of the finite world it proposes to invoke).

To begin the presentation of one's views with aprioric affirmations and an appeal to faith is no more irrational or intellectually disreputable in theology than it is in philosophy or in natural science.

Experimentation and observation get nowhere apart from tacit presuppositions. Empirical science must routinely take for granted what it cannot prove, including such principles as the comprehensive unity, harmony, and intelligibility of the universe, the prevalence of some kind of causal continuity in nature, and the necessity of honesty in experimentation and in scientific research. Without antecedently assuming such postulates, empirical science cannot even get under way. No physicist can prove that real affinity exists between his theories and the objective condition of nature. The scientific explanation of what occurred in the first moment of time depends upon an act of faith, namely, upon confidence in the principle of uniformity.

Critical demotion of Christian theology from its earlier status as a science was long based on the misleading notion that genuine science avoids presuppositions. Modern empirical scientists at first boldly professed to be assumption-free. But once it became evident that no science can exist without presuppositions, modernist critics argued that, rather than simply inheriting its presuppositions as sacrosanct, science at least questions its presuppositions and stands ready to test and revise them. Orthodox Christians simply accommodate hoary tradition as truth, critics implied, whereas only the empirical method of laboratory observation and verification can validate truth claims; thus modern science affords Christian supernaturalism no comfort.

Theological evidentialists, no less than other theologians, begin with aprioric assumptions. The evidentialist may be less disposed than his fellow theologians to admit that his mind harbors presuppositions, but even the faulty presupposition that ideally the case for God is set forth without presuppositions invalidates his disavowal of operative assumptions. The fact is, nothing will set the mind adrift more fruitlessly than the absence of all postulates; indeed, such absence leads to mindlessness in less time than it takes to think. In short, without faith neither science nor philosophy nor theology can make progress.

To engage in authentic truth Christianity need not subscribe to secular statements of how we must ideally conduct theological inquiry. The Christian religion is not obliged antecedently to accept extraneous theories of truth or to accommodate its own alternative to them as the price of earnest metaphysical elaboration and discussion. Christians need not vindicate Christian tenets and remove them from secular suspicion by submitting to restrictive criteria and squaring them with rival views imperiously asserted by neo-Kantians, logical positivists, existentialists, or others. To establish the "credibility" of Christian inquiry by first exhibiting its compatibility with alien theories is merely to negotiate away Christianity's uniqueness. We give Kantians and positivists liberty to state their assumptions; indeed, we are eager to hear what they say. Christians should similarly present their distinctive view of truth, one that embraces God who creates and illumines our belief-forming mechanisms. Christians should feel no compulsion to taper their transcendent theistic epistemology to the preferences of hostile philosophers.

An intellectual is wholly within the bounds of philosophical and theological legitimacy if he believes God exists and affirms His existence even in the absence of empirical proof. No rational basis exists for limiting credible propositions to only those that involve evidence of the kind that specially impresses physicists or anthropologists. The epistemic propriety of belief in God does not depend on supportive empirical or evidential considerations.

Throughout its long history, philosophy has always recognized the legitimacy of assuming without proof a philosophical axiom or postulational principle as an initial basis of reasoning. Democritus never demonstrated that all substance consists of indivisible and imperceptibly small particles; he postulated this premise and attempted to explain all existence consistently in terms of it. Plato never demonstrated the independent existence of the invisible world of Eternal Ideas; he argued that all lesser existence participates in or mirrors them. He would likely have dismissed as a Sophist, moreover, anyone who deprived him of a hearing in the absence of empirical proof of the existence of Eternal Ideas.

In trying to explain the whole of reality and life, the history of philosophy revolves in large measure around comprehensive explanatory principles postulated by a succession of philosophers. The secular theories rivaling

Christian theism are notably divergent and unstable. Many are self-referentially incoherent. They fail to meet even the epistemic standards or tests that their sponsors propose for distinguishing truth from untruth; that is, they cannot even justify their own basic principles by the specified criteria. Their speculations about truth and verification therefore are not to be regarded as self-evidently authoritative; they merely enjoy conventional acceptance.

Kant, for example, did not derive his transcendental forms of thought through his epistemic theory, which identified all knowledge as a joint product of sense content and a priori forms. Since the a priori forms were not sense perceptible, Kant must have postulated them independently of the theory.

There is no way that the philosophical naturalist can "prove" the declared truth of his scientistic worldview other than by relying on his theory's own assumptions. The evidence long cited—namely, that the theory "works"—is widely disputed by those who observe that scientism has in fact failed us since it offers no meaningful view either of the future, or of morality, or of purpose.

At long last modern science itself recognizes the prior importance of theoretical models for interpreting empirical data. In this respect Frederick Suppe has provided a helpful overview of how changes in recent modern scientific thought have eventuated.[3] From 1920 to 1950, scientific theory was largely dominated by Logical Positivism and empirical analysis, which disowned claims for true scientific theory; scientific hypotheses were seen as serviceable only for predicting observable phenomena. Then, between 1950 and 1970, when scientific theory was not yet declared finally explanatory and definitive but simply historical and culturally relative, comprehensive scientific worldviews emerged nonetheless through the cosmologies of influential philosophers of science like Thomas Kuhn, Paul Feyerabend, and Stephen Toulmin. It was between 1970 and 1977, however, in the so-called era of "critical-historical realism," that scientific claims became more specifically dogmatic. Cosmologists spoke more confidently of unobservable transcendent entities; they claimed larger explanatory powers, moreover, and pursued possibilities of affirming true scientific theory. In the present decade, however, worldview perspectives have once again become sociologically and historically oriented. Scientific theory now employs conjectural models and generously invokes analogy and metaphor, although the possibility of empirical falsification is recognized and accepted as a characteristic of authentic empirical science.

Alongside these shifting scientific perspectives William A. Rottschaefer monitors a parallel movement of religious viewpoints.[4] He correlates empirical investigation with critical realism, that is, with the view that experimentation—whether naturalistic or theistic—yields both cognitive understanding of external reality and increasing explanatory power. Concentrating on religious experience, he concludes that science and religion alike have an epistemic character.

Such a view is continually challenged by scientific naturalists, for whom frequently changing scientific theory is more instrumental than objectively cognitive and explanatory. But, say religious theists, whatever else we may derive from religious experience, the fact remains that the articles of the Apostles' Creed were not distilled from universal experience. They add, moreover, that ongoing, enlarging experience can accommodate no unrevisable finalities. By contrast, Christian theists affirm a Christological reality that is "the same yesterday, today, and forever" and a faith "once for all delivered."

Fathered by Schleiermacher, theological modernism regarded scientific empiricism as the reliable way of knowing and consequently demeaned the miraculous as unscientific and prescientific. It anchored the case for God in universal religious experience. One result was that, while affirming God's existence, modernism disavowed finality in defining God's nature. To shift attestation of Christian core doctrines to empirical considerations, as the evidentialists do, carries high risks. One makes an unfulfillable claim for empirical and historical science, moreover, if in a quest for demonstrable certainty one expects from its methodology more than high probability. Is the Christian view of God and the world really well served by methodology that, at best, can affirm with 95 percent probability that Jesus died for sinners or 90 percent probability that He arose bodily from the grave?

We have said that a speculative metaphysician who postulates an explanatory first principle may well dismiss as quite arbitrary any requirement that he first provide some external empirical legitimacy for his principle as a price to be paid in advance for the right to project his controlling axiom. Even in twentieth-century science, important developments have emerged through creative projections when scholars, instead of extrapolating their explanatory postulates from empirical observation, have simply applied creative postulates to the data at hand. Some of the most dramatic progress occurs when new cognitive assumptions displace long-entrenched theories. It is irrelevant to an axiom's explanatory power whether or not its sponsor has arrived at it by empirical observation, philosophical conjecture, religious meditation, private revelation, or even by what he or she considers merely a hunch.

The Christian's primary ontological axiom is the one living God, and his primary epistemological axiom is divine revelation. On these basic axioms depend all the core beliefs of Biblical theism, including divine creation, sin and the Fall, the promise and provision of redemption, the Incarnation of God in Jesus of Nazareth, the regenerate Church as a new society, and a comprehensive eschatology.

Yet a metaphysical view that professes to make sense of all reality and life and involves a universal truth claim must adduce some epistemological justification if it is to escape dismissal as fideism or sheer faith that derogates reason.

Augustine's discussion of truth that is sponsored by faith is preceded by an intellectual search for truth; rational inquiry exposes the need to accept certain basic beliefs or principles by faith. Augustine recognizes the need, moreover, to show that his commitments are not illogical. For Augustine, faith is the mind's way of knowing. It is thinking in view of a higher divine revelatory authority reinforced by assent of the will. Faith is a certitude that, in the light of that higher authority, probes and analyzes what is believed and stipulates its content.

Only by careful attention to the role of presuppositions will the disaster of suspending Christian truth upon empirical considerations be avoided. Every effort to talk authoritatively about God simply on the ground of sense perception or of human experience is vulnerable and doomed. Schleiermacher argued for God's reality on the basis of man's sense of absolute dependence, but critics were quick to indicate that human experience is a commentary not on theology but on anthropology. Empirical method deals with phenomenal, not with noumenal, reality; it cannot adjudicate the existence and nature of the supernatural. Worse yet, it yields only tentative and revisable conclusions; it cannot provide an irreversible verdict on anything. To rest the case for Christianity on an empirical appeal is not only methodologically unpromising but also theologically hazardous.

Yet the evangelical presuppositionalist does not accept the characterization of his axioms as arbitrary. The Christian believer knows assuredly that his postulates and control beliefs are not conjecturally grounded, but are anchored in the triune God's self-existence and self-disclosure. The Christian knows God to be the source of all truth; truth is what God thinks and says. Christianity has never been embarrassed by the centrality of the *Logos* in the Trinity; *Logos* and Wisdom are intrinsic to the Godhead. The Christian affirms his axioms to be presuppositions fundamental to all thought and being; they are basic to human noetic structure. Every human being ought to assume these axioms, he contends, in order to account for the reality and intelligibility of existence. He insists that his explanatory principles are grounded ultimately and eternally in the *Logos* of God. The Christian doctrine of creation, he emphasizes, offers a transcendent guarantee of the unity, orderliness, intelligibility, and stability of natural processes; it also provides a basis for belief that some rational overlap exists between explanatory images and the objects of experimentation.

The Christian knows, moreover, that it is only by divine grace that he believingly participates in the epistemic and ontic realities affirmed by the Biblical heritage.

Yet he does not contend that the truth of Christianity is or can be known only by those who are converted. An atheist or an agnostic, a pantheist or a deist—if attentive to the data—can grasp the essential Christian doctrines simply by reading the Bible. The substitutionary Atonement and bodily Resurrection of Jesus, the divine forgiveness of sins and humanity's need of the new birth for participation in the Kingdom of God, are credal affirmations that even schoolchildren can understand. Evangelical orthodoxy does not hold that one must first appropriate Biblical truth in order to understand it. Were that the case, Bible distribution, evangelism, and apologetics would make little sense. Quite to the contrary, the Bible warns of approaching divine punishment for deliberate neglect of spiritual truth that humans know even in a state of unregeneracy.

To be sure, many schools of non-Biblical thought vigorously oppose the Christian view of God and the world. The history of philosophy offers many rival first principles —from Democritean atoms to Leibnizian monads to the

Hegelian Absolute, from Darwinian earth-evolution by slow, gradual, almost imperceptible change to Hoyle's primitive genes that emerge from a stellar soup and ride on the tails of comets to invade our cosmos. The history of religions likewise offers many global alternatives, from Hinduism's impersonal world-soul Brahma to Iranian Shi'ite fundamentalism, from So'ka Gakkai principles in Japan to New Age enthusiasm in America, and much else.

Many of these faith options have no interest whatever in objective and eternal truth. By no means do all religions or philosophies exert a universal truth claim. Those appealing only to subjective decision or considering truth to be culturally relative, or those mystically transcending a distinction between truth and falsehood, cannot even legitimately make truth claims.

Logical inconsistency embarrasses the claims of any speculative system and does so most destructively when basic principles appear unstable. Logical positivists postulate that only premises verifiable by sense data can be meaningful or true. But in that case this very premise—itself empirically unverifiable—cannot be considered meaningful or true. "Theology of revolution" proponents look to the Hebrew exodus from Egyptian oppression as a paradigm and Biblical legitimation for using violence to promote social change. But since revolution proponents embrace critical views of Scripture, on what ground can they authoritatively invoke the Exodus record? What's more, the Hebrews never overthrew the Egyptian government; their strength lay not in violence but in spiritual obedience to Yahweh.

Although the notion is current in ecumenical inter-faith circles that revelation is found in all religions, the fact is that a doctrine of rational divine disclosure is highly uncommon among world religions and world philosophies, much more uncommon than *Religionsgeschichte* scholars would have us believe. It is noteworthy that among all the great world faiths, only Judaism, Christianity, and Islam affirm "the speaking God"; insofar as Islam affirms this, moreover, dependency on the prior Judeo-Christian Biblical heritage is indisputable.

There can be no decisive choice between alternatives if we disavow any external referent by which to judge truth claims. The crucial question is not whether a scholar must begin with faith; the critical question, rather, is whether such faith is nonrational belief. Are public reason and evidence at all relevant to theological truth claims and, if so, just what is their role?

In appealing to transcendent revelation as its basic epistemic axiom, Christianity casts its truth claim comprehensively over all areas of human life. The fact that Christianity postulates first principles and affirms fixed core beliefs does not rule out the propriety of rational tests. Neither does the appropriateness of a rational test imply that Christianity must be regarded as only hypothesis.

A telling external test of universal validity and of truth is logical consistency. Logical inconsistency sacrifices plausibility; a logically inconsistent system cannot be valid or true. Logical consistency may not decisively establish the truth of intellectual claims, but it is nonetheless a potent negative test.

God's self-revelation is intelligible disclosure; divine revelation is a mental activity. The speaking God—who makes His nature and will known in intelligible propositional statements—articulates truth verbally. Consistency is a divine perfection. In convicting human beings of their sinfulness, the Holy Spirit uses truth as the means of persuasion. Ultimately, regenerate humanity will be fully conformed to the mind and holiness of Christ.

Evangelical orthodoxy therefore has no cause to shun logic; it has every reason to openly exhibit premises that derive consistently from its basic axioms—namely, divine creation of the world and of human beings in God's image; humanity's dominion over the cosmos and stewardship of it; the Fall of Adam and his posterity into moral revolt; the divine offer of redemption to penitent sinners; Yahweh's covenant with Israel and His punitive exile of the Hebrews; the merciful gift of salvation through Jesus Christ, who, as the risen Crucified One, heads a regenerate new society; the Church's global mission of evangelism and promotion of social justice; the imminent return of Christ in final judgment on humanity and the nations; the vindication of righteousness and complete rout of evil; and mankind's dual destiny predicated on individual spiritual and moral response.

A routine evidentialist complaint against presuppositionalists is that they are locked up within their assumptions, whereas evidentialists are concerned about external evidence. But this complaint is as fallacious as is the evidentialist insistence that evidentialists are assumption-free. By no means do all presuppositionalists consider evidence

irrelevant to faith claims, any more than all presuppositionalists consider faith hostile to reason. Presuppositionalists
insist that relevant objective evidence exists externally to
the basic Christian axioms and their implications. That evidence is not, to be sure, empirical data of the sort on which
evidentialists rely in trying to demonstrate God's existence
from the not-God. Rather, the decisive evidence is inspired
Scripture; the Bible is Christian theology's authoritative
verifying principle.

By sense observation it is impossible to prove that
God created the universe *ex nihilo*; that all human beings
bear the image of God; that all humanity is guilty in Adam;
that Jesus was born of a virgin and lived sinlessly in the
days of His flesh; that He died for the sins of humanity; that
after crucifixion He arose bodily, never to die again, and is
the firstfruits of a general resurrection to come; and that
human beings are destined for an afterlife involving an awe-
some dual destiny in eternity. Such doctrines are not empirically derivable; they are confirmed by the inspired
Scriptural teaching.

The most noteworthy reliance by evidentially minded
theologians on empirical factors lies in their promoting of
"proofs"—some would prefer to say more modestly, "evidences"—for God's existence. Although these arguments
share much in common with Thomas Aquinas's so-called
fivefold proof, Protestant circles usually identify them as the
cosmological, teleological, and anthropological arguments.
These formulations begin with the universe—that is, the
cosmos and man—and proceed inductively to God as the
personal, intelligible, moral cause of all finite existence.

Contrary to Thomas, even most empirically oriented evangelicals concede that the "proofs" are not logically demonstrable; they contend, rather, that the "evidences" indicate the high probability of God's existence, a probability so overwhelming as to render human unbelief immoral.

I shall not here repeat criticisms of this view already detailed in *God, Revelation and Authority*, Volume 1.[5] The evidentialist effort is a variant of natural theology. But if the "proofs" are conclusively demonstrative, they lead to a divine reality that is less or other than the God of the Bible. One cannot make a decisive case for infinite Deity simply by extension from the not-God; by beginning with finite existence and paying strict attention to logical procedures one will arrive at the infinite only by a quantum leap of non-rational faith. Thus, however much evidentialism invests its empirical proofs with the aura of reason, it unwittingly falls under the same judgment that it gratuitously passes on presuppositionalism—namely, that of championing faith without reason. Like Thomism, evidentialism introduces divine revelation into the discussion too late to be serviceable. This is not to dismiss cosmic order and human reason and conscience as of no significance for theism; the emphasis on design and rationality and morality may have quite other uses than that of demonstrating the existence of God.

Worse yet, many evangelical empiricists now confuse general revelation with natural theology. They channel texts bearing on God's universal revelation in nature and history and conscience to support the highly debatable view that, despite the Fall, there survives in all humanity a shared body of theological and moral doctrine. This theory not only glosses the cognitive divergences but also presupposes too optimistic a view of humanity's condition after the Fall.

That the living God continues to reveal Himself universally in nature and history and in and to the mind and conscience of man is not here in debate. Nor is the lucidity of that universal revelation in doubt, or its potency in actually and everywhere penetrating human reason and conscience. We are not to fault the universal divine revelation as epistemically flawed. There is in divine revelation no inherent necessity for its epistemic distortion.

The fault, rather, lies with humanity. The frustration of general divine revelation is due to obstinate and unstable human volition. In the very reception of God's revelation, fallen and rebellious human beings will "down" and suppress that revelation; they twist, warp, and taper it to what is more compatible and congenial with an alienated will. This rebellious intellectual response is attested among intellectuals by the multiform history of philosophy and, even more generally, by the multiple world religions and their many private faiths.

Yet, through the *imago Dei* given at creation every human person gains an ineradicable awareness that God exists and that other selves and the external world exist. Every human self, to begin with, knows to be genuine and inescapable a distinction between God and the not-God, a distinction between good and evil, and a distinction between truth and falsehood. Every human being is aware, moreover, that knowing truth and the good puts one in touch with divinity. Not only do all human beings share these formal aspects of the *imago*, however, but also they know instinctively and intuitively that God does in fact exist, that the world really exists, and that other selves actually exist. A Christian theist does not need inductive arguments to know that God exists, or that he himself exists, or that the cosmos and other selves exist.

In thought and conscience, moreover, every human being stands unavoidably and perpetually in divine-human relationships that carry some awareness of God's nature and essential goodness and truth. The *imago Dei* not only has formal content; it also has material content. No one is wholly without light, and every human self is culpable for revolt against light.

Given the human self's volitional rebellion, the light of general revelation may in different contexts survive in different patterns and intensities, depending upon the degree and depth of human animosity. But revelation has an inextinguishable presence nonetheless, one that renders the human species morally and spiritually culpable for revolt against the Deity.

In view of fallen humanity's fluctuating and fleeting spiritual relationships, the quest for certainty is unpromising. It is doubly misguided when one turns to empirical and experiential considerations as the ground of faith or as demonstrable proof. Almost all human day-to-day concerns are settled within the realm of probabilities; probability is the rule of life. Even our legal system in its judgment of criminals relies upon circumstantial evidence.

Yet we thirst for more than mere probability in respect to human destiny. Christian theology meets the demand for certainty with a reminder that certainty has no necessary connection with truth; it can be more emotional or volitional than cognitive. Some persons have certainty about the precise date of the Lord's return; others are certain that eating grapefruit relieves migraine, or that vinegar cures warts. The Christian faith offers not mathematical or speculative certainty, but rather spiritual assurance. Divine authority eliminates the rational gap between probability and certainty. Such assurance is grounded not in empirical probabilities but in a supernatural witness of the Holy Spirit that individually enlivens objectively inspired Scripture. The Spirit uses truth as an instrument of persuasion, truth attested by Scripture and testable for logical consistency.

Christianity therefore fears nothing from public reason; it is neither fideistic nor empiricistic nor rationalistic. Christianity has no less right to affirm its ultimate explanatory principles than do other world- and-life-views. One who is persuaded on other grounds needs neither empirical nor existential nor speculative arguments to state his case. To imply that one is submental if one defends theism without first subscribing to the demands of empiricism or of some other *ism* is to indulge in propaganda rather than to exercise logic.

As revelationally grounded and intelligible faith, Christianity sets out from the ontological priority of the living God and the epistemological priority of divine revelation. From these basic postulates it derives and expounds all the core doctrines of the Christian religion. Among these is the divine gift of saving faith that enlists the entire self in love, worship, and obedient service of the infinite Creator and Judge of mankind and the nations. Deductive theology invites the attention of nonbelievers to logical consistency as a negative test of truth and to Scriptural verification. The claims of deductive theology are intelligible to any person who heeds logic, whether or not he or she is personally a believer. But as one of its doctrines, Christianity affirms the Spirit of Truth as the dynamic reality whereby the living God sovereignly nurtures saving faith in the life of the penitent. The Christian can hold both head and heart high if on his own ground—and quite independently of Plato or Aristotle or Hume or Hegel—he says with Paul, "I know whom I have believed, and am convinced . . ." (2 Timothy 1:12).

THREE

The Axioms of Biblical Theism

Every theology or philosophy or science has a starting point enabling it to get under way.

Euclid's classic work on *The Elements*, written about 300 B.C., stated the five postulates or unproved principles concerning lines, angles, and figures from which he deduced geometry. Euclid postulated, for example, that between any two points we can draw a straight line, and that all right angles are equal to each other. Besides the five postulates he adduced five other unproved principles, called axioms. The postulates deal specifically with geometrical concerns, while the axioms deal more generally with magnitude. Modern mathematicians and logicians now use the terms *axiom* and *postulate* interchangeably.

From his postulates, axioms, and definitions, Euclid deduced the theorems that state the content of plane and solid geometry. Later geometricians disputed certain of Euclid's theorems and debated whether Euclid's geometry is based on necessary truths or empirical hypotheses. Yet even the geometries of N. I. Lobachevsky and of G. F. B. Riemann are formally consistent with Euclidean geometry and can be given a Euclidean model. "Any hypothesis, prediction, or explanation that can be expressed in one of these descriptive schemes," comments Stephen F. Barker, "can be expressed just as accurately in the other."[1]

Philip Kitcher contends that mathematical knowledge is essentially empirical; that is, that its truths and proofs are experientially grounded.[2] But his arguments are unpersuasive. As Joseph W. Dauben notes, Kitcher merely leaps over the difficulties of empiricist approaches to mathematics: he ignores many recent works (e.g., by Bos, Barn, Grabiner, Fleckenstein, Hofmann, Manning, Scriba, Westfall, Whiteside) simply on the ground that they are "biased" aprioristically.[3]

Just as geometry has basic axioms from which its theorems flow, so theological and philosophical systems also have governing axioms. Axioms are the ruling principles with which any system of thought begins. They are never deduced or inferred from other principles, but are simply presupposed. No axiom is arrived at by reasoning; as the starting point, an axiom is therefore in the nature of the case beyond proof.

Logic itself rests on empirically unprovable principles that one must assume in every effort to communicate intelligibly—e.g., the principle of noncontradiction.

From its controlling axioms every system's theorems are subsequently deduced. Even if empiricists may and do deny it, all systems are based on axioms; without initial axioms nothing can be demonstrated. Natural science is impossible unless one assumes that meaningful correspondence exists between the laws of thought and the order of the external world.

In philosophy the axiom that underlies naturalistic atheism is that physical process and events comprise the whole of reality. Empiricism rests on the axiom that all knowledge has its source in sensation alone. Kant's governing axiom is that knowledge is a joint product of innate forms and sense content. Logical Positivism sets out from the axiom that only sentences verifiable by sense experience can be true or meaningful.

Empiricism cannot empirically justify its governing premise. From sense experience, to which he professed to limit the content of all knowledge, Kant could not derive information about innate forms of thought. Since Logical Positivism cannot sensually verify its own verificatory thesis, it cannot exempt itself from meaninglessness.

Each worldview has its distinctive starting point or touchstone thesis through which it attempts to unify and explain human experience. The Christian philosopher is under no intellectual compulsion, therefore, to accept rival premises, however fashionable, as the starting point for advancing his or her theistic worldview. And the nonbeliever cannot object that the axioms of Christian theism are derived from a source other than sense experience or mystical intuition or philosophical conjecture. The evangelical's confidence that Biblical theism is comprehensively explanatory is as legitimate a pre-philosophical assumption for formulating his or her truth claim as is the logical positivist's notion that only empirical confirmability rescues the term *God* from meaninglessness.

What distinguishes Christian axioms from rival axioms is not that Christian axioms are a priori; all axioms are. "No one can consistently object," writes Gordon H. Clark, "to Christianity's being based on a nondemonstrable axiom. If the secularists exercise their privilege of basing their theorems on axioms, then so can Christians. If the former refuse to accept our axioms, then they can have no logical objection to our rejecting theirs."[4]

Christian philosophers are ill-advised if, to make Biblical theism as palatable as possible to secular philosophers, they conform Christian claims to the alien and often hostile principles of non-Biblical thinkers. The validity of Christian theism does not depend on whether unbelievers find its presuppositions acceptable, or upon espousing only those beliefs that dissenting philosophers approve. As Alvin Plantinga puts it, "[T]he Christian philosopher is entirely within his rights in starting from belief in God. . . . He has a right to take the existence of God for granted and go on from there in his philosophical work just as other philosophers take for granted the existence of the past, say, or of other persons, or the basic claims of contemporary physics."[5]

Plantinga rejects even the notion of some Christian philosophers that they should engage with atheistic or agnostic philosophers "in a common search for the correct philosophical positions *vis-a-vis* the question whether there is such a person as God," as if the Christian philosopher must show from their premises that his view is probable or justified.[6]

The contemporary secular philosopher often insists that the pursuit of scientific or historical knowledge requires scholars to look critically at all beliefs, but then proceeds to take his own assumptions for granted and demands that others revise their suppositions to conform to his.

But the Christian philosopher need not taper his con-

victions to those of an antagonist as the price of philosophical engagement. In Plantinga's words: "The Christian
philosopher quite properly *starts from* the existence of God,
and presupposes it in philosophical work, whether or not he
can show it to be probable or plausible with respect to
premises accepted by all philosophers, or most philosophers
at the great contemporary centers of philosophy."[7] He has a
right and even a duty to state his case on his own ground
whether skeptical contemporaries believe it or not. If he
does not do so, he merely throws his case away. Rather than
being intimidated by brash demands of those who grant no
plausibility to Christian principles and who insist that we
applaud only propositions amenable to an entrenched, non-
Christian philosophical establishment, it is wholly legitimate for the Christian philosopher to begin with what he
knows as a Christian.

The Christian ought to systematize, deepen, and
apply his pre-philosophical convictions in order to test them
for explanatory power and logical consistency. Even empirical scientists postulate conceptual models in their efforts to
account for the cosmos. They long spoke of "laws" of
nature, but if their numerous formulas were really grounded
in nature, scientists would not have needed constantly to
revise them. They long spoke of causality, but causes are
beyond empirical verifiability; consequently, scientists now
speak more guardedly of predictable consequences.

According to Huston Smith, the basic assumption of
the contemporary worldview is that "reality is unordered in
any objective way that man's mind can discern."[8] Much
current commentary assumes either that the external or tran-

scendent world is intrinsically unstructured or that man contributes creatively and decisively to our knowledge of it. On this approach, ultimate principles are pursued for their utility or fruitfulness rather than for their objective truth.

It is theoretically as legitimate for a theist to view God as the cause (perhaps the final cause) of the universe as for an atheist to view nature as a chaos that man "orders."

The basic axioms of the Christian religion are two. The basic ontological axiom is *the living God*; the basic epistemological axiom is *divine revelation*. These axioms can be stated more fully and precisely, as when the triune God is said to be the basic ontological axiom and revelatory truths are declared the basic epistemological axiom. These axioms imply each other. Without the living God there would be no divine revelation. Without intelligible self-disclosure we would not know that God exists.

Building on Ian Barbour's views, Avery Dulles speaks of theological models much as philosophers of science speak of theoretical models.[9] Barbour contrasts imaginatively projected scientific-theoretical models with scientific-experimental models used in laboratories; the former, he notes, are creative interpretive models for dealing with what is not observable.[10] Theoretical models, Barbour stresses, fail to represent reality literally. Yet such distinction is artificial. The fact is that physics, too, is operational; none of the laws of physics is a fixed truth. Generally all science is similarly operational, since scientific conclusions and affirmations about the physical world are but tentative and revisable.

If theological models merely fall into this same class,

then the truth of theological affirmations remains in doubt. Norman Malcolm notes that "present-day academic philosophers are far more prone to challenge the credentials of religion than of science."[11] Much recent religious thought considers theological interpretation intrinsically tentative and views theology as a creative enterprise doomed to perpetual revision. It assumes that in theology no decisive explanatory model can be offered or should be expected.

Postulating Christian theism as a theoretical model alongside other theoretical models need not imply, however, that Christianity is merely a speculative construct imaginatively projected to account for man and the world. Many non-Christians doubtless view Biblical theism as simply a conjectural way of thinking about life and existence. All speculative thinkers tend to regard rival views in pejorative terms, while they applaud their own alternative. Yet Christianity does not affirm its axioms simply as a provisional theoretical approach to an intrinsically meaningless external world or postulate them only for their utility; it holds that axioms illumine reality literally and factually.

The Christian insists that the Biblical doctrine of revelation is not an achievement of philosophical reasoning. "If revelation were not necessary to know what revelation was," Dulles aptly remarks, "revelation, it would seem, would not be necessary at all."[12] C. S. Lewis puts it another way: Christianity is "a religion you could not have guessed."[13] The Christian knows that the axioms of his faith are grounded in transcendent realities and not in speculative fabrication. The Biblical view is that human reason has no normative, creative role in respect to truth. God is truth and the fountain of all truth. In the Christian view, God's mind and will are the source of all truth, of mathematics, of logic, of law, and of cosmic order.

The negative impulse of the Enlightenment aimed to promote human reason by stifling supernatural revelation. As Reinhold Niebuhr remarks, "Humanistic rationalism, forgetting that human reason as well as human physical existence is a derived, dependent/created and finite reality, makes it into a principle of interpretation of the meaning of life."[14] But the Enlightenment managed to suffocate both reason and revelation, instead of recognizing that reason is the ally and not the enemy of divine revelation. That firm feature of modern philosophy is now looked upon with increasing suspicion, and, as Nicholas Wolterstorff senses, scholars "are willing to ask anew about the relation between reason and revelation."[15]

Although the terms *postulate* and *axiom* are often used interchangeably, the former is sometimes applied loosely to the essential tenets or doctrines that flow from the basic axioms. So in *The Christian View of God and The World* James Orr, sketching the major Biblical doctrines, wrote of postulates of the Christian view such as God, nature and man, and sin.[16] On the basis of special divine disclosure Christianity promulgated its doctrines of the existence of a supernatural Sovereign, of creation *ex nihilo*, of man's divine image and stewardship of the earth, of man's violated relationship with his Maker, of God's salvation of His fallen creatures, of His special inspiration of prophets and apostles, of His Incarnation in Jesus of Nazareth, of the role of the Church in the world, and of mankind's dual destiny in eternity.

Over against the Christian affirmation of revelation as the basic epistemological axiom, secular philosophers project rival explanatory principles. Empiricists exalt observation and experience above philosophical reasoning as a way of knowing; yet even empiricists are at odds with each other. Many hail the modern scientific method—sense observation and verification—as definitive of reality. Strict empiricists question the reality of the supernatural, since metaphysical and moral concerns fall outside empirical purview. Others widen the meaning of experience beyond sensate knowledge to embrace direct relationships to other selves and to God. An "encounter" theology grounds belief in God's reality in inner divine-human confrontation. Mystics appeal to immediate experience in behalf of a god beyond good and evil, beyond truth and error, and outside time and space. Experience is clearly not self-interpreting; interpretation is often colored by the prevailing religious, philosophical, and cultural outlook. Nor are our experiences self-authenticating or infallible. Shall we then dismiss all religious and philosophical beliefs as culturally relative?

Some say that religious experience is inexpressible in language. But in that case nobody else can be urged to have the same experience. If experience is indefinable, does one really know what it is? Propositional expressibility is, of course, a precondition for evaluating any system. A system that is not propositionally expressible involves no shareable truth claims and can in no way be tested. Even so, can we in any case have another person's experience? Or does that query merely hide behind the egocentric predicament and imply only that an experience must be mine if I am to have it? In any event, experience is incomplete and vulnerable to continual supplementation and correction. Some religions, moreover—notably Judaism and Christianity—insist that God does not relate Himself to the universe or even to all human beings in wholly uniform ways. Can anyone then really tell the unqualified truth about God speaking on the basis only of one's personal experience?

In earlier generations, empiricists held that explanatory hypotheses arise out of accumulated experiential data and inductive principles, which further experience can in turn then verify. But we do not and cannot directly experience the physical world; our experiential data consists of sensations and neurological impulses. The cause of these sensations, however, was held to be the physical world. The argument for the existence of other selves—human and divine—was based similarly upon inferences from our conscious experiences.

Empirical argument frequently moves from the data of experience to realities or facts beyond experience; moreover, it attributes to these transcendent entities qualities not experientially observed. The physicist argues from meter readings in cloud chambers to subatomic particles, or from the design of nature to an omnipotent divine Architect. But he has as little immediate empirical experience of atoms as he does of God.

The "proofs" of God's existence proceeded from the orderliness of nature, or from a perceived pattern of historical events (whether exceptional or recurrent). This line of argument was increasingly undermined, most effectively by David Hume. Hume argued that empirical data cannot establish either the existence of God, the existence of causes, the existence of the physical world, or even the existence of one's own selfhood.

Worse yet, as Hume noted, the empirical argument to an omnipotent Designer covertly assumes that the universe originated by creation. But the exclusion of other possibilities of origin is unjustified unless one has had prior experience of the origin of worlds. Moreover, the fact of evil in the world might indicate a finite rather than an infinite God. Design in nature might also be the work of multiple spiritual powers. (Darwin later suggested chance variation and natural selection.)

Although there is no philosophical consensus on how we must define experience, the limits of scientific empiricism (or laboratory observation) are now so widely recognized that strict empiricists concede that the method can provide no verdict on theological entities and moral imperatives. Empirical observation deals with the phenomenal, with our sense perceptions of reality. Standard inductive techniques do not allow us to go beyond perceived data.

But what occasions our sense perceptions? The desk looks like a solid object, yet physicists say that it is comprised of imperceptible events. Bertrand Russell remarked that "if we cannot be sure of the independent existence of other 'people's' bodies, and therefore still less of other people's minds . . . it may be that the whole outer world is nothing but a dream, and that we alone exist."[17]

In examining empirical "proofs" for God's existence, many professors in philosophy of religion courses declare either that God does not exist or that, if He does, He differs remarkably from the God of the Bible. No theist should be stunned by modern declarations of the invalidity of the so-called theistic proofs. The significance of empirical philosophical arguments, insofar as they are constructive, is not that they demonstrably prove God's existence, but that they may remove obstacles to unbelief. No so-called proof of God's existence engenders faith. Neither experience nor history provides a truly comprehensive view of reality; both remain open to tomorrow. A consistent explanatory system cannot be attained by any empirical method.

Basic beliefs are not empirically inferred. We screen experiential data through cognitive lenses; we do not grasp sense data as bare or neutral data. We comprehend our experience in the context of an interpretive framework of beliefs, of framework principles, or of a foundational world-picture that we bring to experience and within which, as a *Weltbild* or background system, to quote Ludwig Wittgenstein, "all testing, all confirmation and disconfirmation of an hypothesis, takes place."[18]

The decisive role of presuppositions is increasingly apparent to twentieth-century scientific scholarship. The great advances in recent modern scientific theory have arisen through creative postulation rather than inductive observation. As Lesslie Newbigin says, "[T]he formula *credo ut intelligam* is fundamental to science."[19] Contemporary physics speaks of theoretical constructs like Big Bang, subatomic particles, and magnetic field not on the basis of experimental induction but on the basis of intuition and imagination. "A scientist's *methods* may be completely empirical," writes Stephen Toulmin, "yet his investigations will have no direction without the guidance of a pre-existing body of ideas."[20] Deductions from creative hypotheses undergo subsequent laboratory testing, and their credibility depends upon a range of confirmation or disconfirmation.

Empirical theories are always accepted in the absence of empirical *proof*. Often they gain currency even before impressive empirical verification is available. Sometimes scientists even affirm existences before there is any empirical observation of them at all (e.g., an extended list of subatomic particles; black holes).

Physicists routinely speak of "seeing" subatomic particles. But, as Richard Morris remarks, what they really observe is hydrogen bubbles. These they equate with particles that are "too small to be observed directly, even by the most powerful electron microscopes. Protons and neutrons, leptons, photons and quarks" are inferred: "physicists believe in them because they can be used to explain so many things that are observed in the laboratory. . . . They are concepts which can be used to codify an enormous amount of data about natural phenomena."[21] Niels Bohr observed a generation ago that, while laboratory readings on pointers and dials are "real," electrons and subatomic particles are useful models.[22]

In 1985 scientists in Zürich developed a new kind of microscope capable of magnifying an object 300 million times and affording them pictures of individual atoms that make up the surface of ordinary objects. The atoms show up as fuzzy balls or little bumps so tiny that 4 billion in a row would measure an inch. Even so, the study of internal components postulated by physicists—a nucleus of protons and neutrons with a cloud of orbiting electrons—still remains to be done. Many physicists in fact hold that electrons exist only as abstractions, as pragmatically useful constructs that enable physicists to systematically present their views of nature. Electrons, in brief, are but postulates or theoretical models that facilitate the experimenter's interpretation of his data.

Logical reflection and creative imagination—some writers call them "a leap into the dark" or "inspired guess-work"—are fully as much and even more at the base of bold new theories in science than are experimental observation and analysis. To be sure, Stephen Toulmin rejects Arthur Koestler's implication that scientists stumble upon their explanations like sleepwalkers and, apart from logical calculation and formal procedures, "make theoretical discoveries by a blind, unreasoning intuition."[23] The fact is that scientific theories are now less often viewed in the context of truth and more often viewed as aesthetic constructs rising from imaginative mystical contemplation through which scholars approach nature and creatively organize its experimental data into an orderly pattern. Richard Morris suggests that theoretical science is not dissimilar to art; it is "an activity that imposes order upon all the myriad aspects of human experience."[24] These theoretical postulations are often accorded more weight than laboratory data, so long as the theories explain relevant phenomena and are capable of adducing some experimental support.

No longer do scientists claim to identify the very "laws of nature." Many speak only of approximations of such laws and some, in view of constantly changing models, wonder to what extent the human mind itself creatively imposes on nature the order we profess to discover. Morris remarks: "There is a sense in which mesons and quarks and gluons are dreams. . . . Do they 'really' exist? they almost certainly do not." Yet "they are real in the sense that they give us a picture of this world that is astonishingly vivid and fruitful. . . . Science seeks to create pictures of the order in nature . . . so logically elegant that we cannot doubt that they are true."[25]

Some Christian scholars use this postulational approach to promote the probable truth of Christianity. D. Elton Trueblood holds that Christian theism as a cognitive principle best accounts for man's scientific, ethical, aesthetic, historical, and religious experience.[26] Biblical theism, he believes, exerts a high probability claim to truth because it offers both an orderly cosmos that science can investigate and an objective moral order. Edward John Carnell affirmed that Christian theism carries a superior truth claim because it accounts logically for the world of existence and experience with greater consistency and coherence than do its intellectual rivals.[27]

David Wolfe warns, however, that Christian theism becomes highly vulnerable if, like scientific postulates, it is conditioned on factors that render it "more or less probable" on the basis of progressive verification. The creeds of Christendom do not affirm a divine Incarnation 60 percent probable, or even a worldview more probable than any alternative. Wolfe insists, and rightly, that Christian belief finds its proper warrant elsewhere.[28]

On the negative side, Wolfe concedes that complete

verification is impossible. But he also stresses Karl Popper's argument that decisive disconfirmation is equally impossible, so that all talk of "degree of verification" or of probability is problematic.[29] In investigating natural and historical data, what constitutes a fact or event and its probability of occurrence (e.g., of a miracle) is not determined apart from the interpreter's theoretical outlook.

One's explanatory beliefs, we have said, are not distilled from uninterpreted data. Rather, our experience itself is made possible by a conceptual apparatus through which we interpret all existence and life. In short, this interpretive framework is what makes experience possible; we locate otherwise nebulous data claims on a metaphysical map.

Belief in God is basic to the Christian view, and no inductive argument from the not-God is necessary to justify it. An intellectual may be well within the bounds of epistemic propriety if he subscribes to God's existence even in the absence of any empirical evidence. In contrast to medieval efforts to justify belief in God's existence on the basis of natural theology, the Protestant Reformers held that belief in God's existence is rational and proper without any philosophical argumentation. They were not on that account fideists; they did not hold that the existence of God is a matter of sheer faith contrary to reason.

Plantinga is right when he insists that the Reformers' belief was not groundless, not epistemically gratuitous or arbitrary, but rationally justifiable. The Reformers stressed God's intelligible self-revelation and the fact of an inescapable human conscience. They contended that, as an aspect of general divine revelation, the truth of God's existence was given in the constitution of human nature. They affirmed that nobody escapes a conviction of the existence of the self-revealing God. A skeptic may take issue with this emphasis. But that disclaimer does not alter the Reformers' insistence that belief in God is epistemically grounded and justifiable and is, moreover, basic to all other truth claims. Neither did the Reformers think it necessary to "prove" the existence of other selves or of the cosmos. Not only is empirical argument unnecessary to establish their existence, but also no such argument is valid.

The crucial issue in regard to Biblical theism is not whether it is right and reasonable to believe contrary to evidence. It is rather the question of just what evidence is appropriate to affirming God's existence. Should one read only the writings of atheists? Or should one confine one's reading to works by philosophers? Or should one read the Bible also and study the life of Jesus? The Bible, notably, begins with the living God; it does not introduce Him belatedly as the conclusion of a syllogism predicated on meticulous observation of the not-God.

To be sure, atheists charge that belief in God's existence is illogical, and some fainthearted theists consider belief in the Judeo-Christian Deity incompatible with the nature of man and the cosmos. Informed scholars will not be quickly overwhelmed by such claims.

In the debate over the ontological status of scientifically unobservable entities, Logical Positivism insisted that theoretical statements about postulated nonobservables must be defined or explicated in terms of observables. The claim that the sentence "God exists" is cognitively vacuous because it cannot be sensually verified was self-referentially destructive; it yielded finally an awareness that Positivism's verification principle discredited Positivism, not theism. Some scientists justified nonobservables not in terms of logical rules but of anticipated behavior or of aesthetics. Other efforts to make logical nonsense of Christian theism, such as the argument that if God is an unembodied spirit He cannot act in the world, rest on philosophical superficiality.

Some analytical philosophers, most notably Alvin Plantinga in America and Peter Geach and Richard Swinburne in Britain, insist that Christianity's central affirmations are logically coherent and rationally defensible. Stephen T. Davis follows Plantinga's emphasis that the Biblical attributes affirmed of God do not render the Judeo-Christian view incoherent.[30]

Every objective worldview affirms that we can know something that everybody else can know and ought to believe. And if we profess to know shareable knowledge, that belief involves us in further relationships to the laws of thought, notably the laws of identity, of non-contradiction, and of excluded middle. Christianity does not disdain the canons of rationality. It offers a comprehensive logical network of beliefs.

Legitimate tests can be applied to the truth claims of the differing metaphysical models that propose to explain all existence and life. The axioms of any system are testable for the consistency or inconsistency with which they account for relevant data. The axioms lose explanatory power if theorems deduced from them are shown to be logically inconsistent.

Contradiction and logical inconsistency have exposed the invalidity of many belief claims. Since logical inconsistency invalidates any syllogism, logical consistency is a negative test of truth.

Against this emphasis on logical consistency even as a negative test of theological truth, John Warwick Montgomery champions empirical verification. In a contingent universe, Montgomery argues, a system as yet undetected may prove to be more consistent than the Christian revelation claim. A demonstration of the logical inconsistency of all extant non-Christian systems does not help much, he insists, since "there can always be, in a contingent universe, system $x + 1$ to contend with," so that the presuppositionalist theologian faces an endless task.[31]

But we can grapple only with known systems; we are not called upon to invent hypothetical consistent alternatives that nobody has as yet postulated. If Montgomery knows a more consistent system than Biblical theism, he should adduce it. The truth of the Christian system is not forced to a tentative status by a failure to examine all sorts of nonexistent imaginative possibilities as potential alternatives. That would indeed be an endless and wholly illegitimate task.

It is too much to expect each of us to evaluate even all existing metaphysical views with equal thoroughness. Yet we should at least investigate captivating options that perennially attract the masses of mankind. Should we not, as Wolfe proposes, investigate the warrant of any scheme that offers "the richest view, the greatest hope, the most powerful values"?[32]

If Christian revelational claims are true, no system will or can be more comprehensively consistent. There may be other and various consistent subsystems (e.g., geometry), but these are all partial. Some fields, notably history, offer little approach to a consistent system. While logic prevails, a consistent system cannot be falsified.

Against a presuppositional approach, empirical theists profess to build their case by appealing not to "opinions" but to "facts." Their appeal to an orderly universe or to Jesus' bodily Resurrection from the dead as demonstrative of God's existence stirs a responsive chord in a believer's heart.

But can an appeal to the "data" of nature or of history, apart from any invocation of divine revelation, provide a logical demonstration of the existence of the Christian God or of the factuality of Jesus' bodily Resurrection? Historical reasoning might conclude that Jesus of Nazareth showed Himself to be indubitably alive after His Crucifixion. But without further appeal to an authoritative Scripture or to God in his revelation, could historical reasoning show that the transcendent Deity had raised Jesus from death never to die again, and raised Him moreover as the firstfruits of an end-time general resurrection?

Montgomery contends that Jesus' Resurrection validates both Jesus' prediction of that event and the event itself as proof of Jesus' divinity. But observational scientists have frequently discovered that empirical validation of prediction is not per se validation of a particular interpretation. A connection assuredly exists between Jesus' divinity and His Resurrection, but that connection is not properly perceived by a theory that the Resurrection as an isolated historical event demonstrably proves Jesus' divinity.

Empiricist criticism of a presuppositional approach loses force once it becomes evident that empiricists are covertly laden with presuppositions of their own. Empirical scientists assume, for example, that time is linear, that the senses provide reliable information, that logic is to be trusted, that valid theories should not contradict each other, that laws operative at one place and time in the universe apply everywhere and always, and that the behavior of the universe is predictable. Such assumptions are not empirically demonstrable; some are in fact parasitic on the Judeo-Christian heritage.

Robert C. Sproul, John H. Gerstner, and Arthur Lindsley decry presuppositionalism and depict it as necessarily fideistic—that is, as appealing for trust prior to and independently of evidence. They do not distinguish types of evidence or do justice to presuppositionalists who strenuously insist on a principle of verification and a test of truth. But more damaging to their own view is the fact that they gloss over presuppositions of their own—namely, the law of non-contradiction, the validity of the law of causality, and the basic reliability of sense perception.[33] Closer attention to the first of these principles—that of non-contradiction—would have raised serious questions about the others, for causality may be understood in several ways. The insistence on cause-and-effect relationships in nature, which the authors apparently have in mind, has long been abandoned by many philosophers and scientists in the interest merely of predictable sequences. To affirm that sense perception is basically reliable is unhelpful unless the authors provide a criterion for distinguishing reliable from unreliable sensations.

Presuppositions decisively influence the interpretation of "data"; the very same experience invites divergent interpretations in keeping with the knower's basic assumptions. Darwin recalled that in earlier days, when he believed in divine Creation rather than in natural selection, the grandeur of the Brazilian forest reinforced his "firm conviction of the existence of God. . . . But now the grandest scenes would not cause any such convictions and feelings to rise in my mind. It may be truly said that I am like a man who has become colour-blind. . . . There seems to be no more design to the variability of organic beings and in the action of natural selection, than in the course in which the wind blows."[34]

The important bearing of presuppositions on the interpretation of empirical data is seen in the different ways that scientists understand the interaction between our planet's atmosphere and the life it sustains, and beyond that, the fitness of these organisms for their diverse environments. Owen Gingerich comments that "the perfect timing of this complex configuration of circumstances is enough to amaze and bewilder many of my friends who look at all this in purely mechanistic terms—the survival of life on earth seems such a close shave as to border on the miraculous. Can we not see here the designer's hand at work?"[35] Even the atheist Sir Frederick Hoyle now regards as the work of "some supercalculating intellect" the nuclear resonance structure of carbon and oxygen and the relative scarcity of carbon, without which human life would be impossible.[36] "Through the eyes of faith," says Gingerich, "one can see numerous vestiges of the designer's hand . . . circumstances of nature impossible to comprehend in the absence of supernatural design. . . . [But] I am doubtful that one can convert a skeptic by the argument of design. . . ."[37] Gingerich affirms that God, Creator and Designer of the universe, "has given us . . . a demonstration of his sacrificial love in the life and death of Jesus" and calls human beings to sacrificial love. "I confess that this is not the logical conclusion of my line of argument; indeed it is the beginning, the point of departure for a way of perceiving science and the universe."[38]

Those who reject the supernatural invert the argument and affirm the anthropic principle; our existence, they contend, shows that the universe sustains us. The "facts" to which evangelical empirical theists appeal are obviously not the "facts" that an empirical naturalist or a process philosopher sees, since "facts" are never neutral or uninterpreted. The premises underlying empirical explanation of the regularities of existence and life are less the product of induction than of creative postulation or of revelatory affirmation in search of confirmation or verification.

The interpretive scheme may have roots in intuition, imagination, tradition, or cultural loading, or it may be grounded in a blend of all these factors. It may be nebulous and inarticulate, or structured and articulate. But, as Wolfe remarks, "Truth claims always involve at least implicit metaphysical assumptions, even when the one who makes them explicitly denies the possibility of metaphysics. The alternative to explicit metaphysics is not neutrality or not metaphysics, but a naive and unexamined metaphysics."[39]

Interpretive presuppositions are now widely regarded as merely subjective or culturally conditioned. If all one's beliefs flow merely from predispositions, then relativism becomes unavoidable if not inevitable. The dogmatic relativist is logically incongruent, moreover, when he tries to exclude his own premises from the net of relativism. If nothing is objectively true, then relativism can hardly propound its own prejudices as true.

The presence of rival worldviews does not imply that none of them is true. One can show that almost all worldviews are internally contradictory or reductionistic or culturally relative without justifying the conclusion that no worldview is objectively true.

The intellectual justification of what we affirm is a critically important matter. Fideism simply affirms its positions authoritatively: it adduces no rational supports and weighs no alternatives; neither does it evaluate the logical consistency of its claims.

On what basis then are we to decide the truth value of divergent interpretive frameworks that claim to make sense of our otherwise disparate and unintegrated experiences? By what warrants shall we assess rival claims? Unless we supply some warrant for our knowledge claims, Wolfe remarks, "our ungrounded belief is easily swayed and abandoned, *even though it might be correct*."[40] Only sufficient warrant for our beliefs can protect us from "changing our minds irrationally or believing irresponsibly."

Validity in logic does not necessarily involve true

conclusions, but knowing that conclusions are true is dependent on formal validity, and no internally inconsistent set of propositions can be true as a whole. When explanations that presume to make sense of existence and life are logically self-contradictory, the truth of those explanations is discredited. Most people, as Frederick Copleston remarks, are "prepared to accept the assumption that . . . we can exclude any theory in so far as it is self-contradictory."[41]

Logical consistency is, however, only a negative test of truth. Self-contradictory premises cannot be true. By exposing logical inconsistency in an interpretive scheme, we call its truth claim in question. But although logical inconsistency invalidates any truth claim, logical consistency does not of itself establish the truth of a particular claim. For a system to be true, more is required than simply not harboring a contradiction. For consistent systems may be elaborated on the basis of rival and mutually exclusive a prioris. Basic premises can be undeviatingly applied, as for example by the theory of naturalistic evolution, and yet not be objectively true. Although a variety of systems may be self-consistent, in no case can a consistent system be arrived at empirically. Our failure to discover contradiction in a system would not assure its truth; the system may not yet be fully enough developed to make its contradictions obvious. One may deduce many theorems from a set of axioms without discovering an inherent contradiction, yet contradiction may still arise several theorems later.

A worldview may even contain some lesser details that are false without its larger claims being invalidated. Containing an identifiable contradiction does not necessarily mean that a theory is false in its entirety. An invalid theory, moreover, may be susceptible of revision that retains its major points, eliminates whatever minor points occasioned the self-contradiction, and renders a new and wholly self-consistent theory. But until and unless it is so revised, the theory can be assumed to be false. In his monumental history of philosophy *Thales to Dewey*, long a standard college text, Gordon H. Clark notes the inconsistencies of even the most prestigious secular thinkers; his survey contains hundreds of references to logic.[42]

The fact that secular axioms sooner or later betray their inability to account consistently for relevant data does not in and of itself prove the Christian revelation to be true. Final verification or demonstrative proof of the truth of any metaphysical overview is presently impossible. But beliefs are philosophically significant only if they are affirmed to be true for all persons, and if warrant for saying so is adduced. In *A Christian View of Men and Things*, Clark patiently examined the claims of contemporary philosophical movements and exhibited their logical deficiencies alongside a presentation of Christian postulates.[43]

There can be but one comprehensive system of truth. If the true system is comprehensive, every false system must contain contradictions.

Some scholars insist on coherence, that is, on the internal relatedness of all statements in a single system of assertions,[44] either as an alternative to consistency as the test of truth or as an additional test of truth. Wolfe, too, emphasizes the need that a conceptual map should constitute a "consistent and coherent system of assertions;"[45]

moreover, to consistency and coherence he adds the factors of comprehensiveness (applicability of the interpretive scheme to all experience) and congruity (appropriateness of the interpretive scheme to the experiences it covers).[46] Yet there is far less difficulty in identifying a valid syllogism than in defining coherence.

Jerry H. Gill proposes three guidelines for escaping erroneous belief systems: comprehensive coherence, internal consistency, and ethical fruitfulness. Clearly the second—which calls for the exclusion of self-contradictory statements and of statements that contradict one's other beliefs—is most important, for without internal consistency the other guidelines collapse. Yet Gill declares absolute consistency "neither possible nor necessary" and, moreover, espouses inherently paradoxic modes of speaking that "bear witness to deep mysteries which are revealing of truth."[47] These concessions seem to rob consistency of decisive importance.

Lesslie Newbigin invites questions when he identifies the superior option not through "logical argument" but rather through "the widest rationality, the greatest capacity to give meaning to the whole of experience," including "faithful endeavors and costly obedience."[48] To be sure, Newbigin recognizes that "no belief system can be faulted by the fact that it rests on unproved assumptions,"[49] and he insists that no "rationally conclusive 'proof'" is in view. But can "the widest rationality" commend an option if it is wide enough to embrace logical contradiction?

"A world-view which is free from internal contradictions is intellectually superior, in this respect," Frederick

Copleston remarks, "to one in which internal contradictions can be detected."[50] "It is improbable that anyone would seriously claim that a logically incoherent theory, simply because of its lack of coherence, is superior to a theory which is logically coherent."[51] "A conception which is self-contradictory is unacceptable, unless we are prepared to consign the ideal of coherence to the dustbin, in which case we had better steer clear of philosophy."[52] A worldview must be comprehensively logical if it is to have comprehensive explanatory power. Copleston says that "the primary use of the criterion of logical coherence is to exclude theories rather than to prove the truth of any particular theory."

Yet coherence means little unless it presupposes consistency; inconsistent coherence could hardly serve even as a negative test of truth. What one scholar considers coherent often seems not so to another, but it is difficult for either of them to dispute the invalidity of a syllogism and even more so to establish the coherence of logically inconsistent principles. A comprehensively consistent system will embrace all other criteria of truth. Coherence is vulnerably jeopardized if it must accommodate illogic. The unity of truth and the insistence that an explanatory theory comport both with underlying axioms and with all relevant data can have no firmer ground than logical consistency.

The argument that the Christian system is circular because it sets out with what needs first to be proved would apply to all systems, since no system exists without basic axioms. The fact is, all arguments involve circularity. Circularity is not a liability; it cannot but be an asset, if all premises mesh in a comprehensive unity of discourse. In a logically consistent system, all propositions comprise a comprehensive unity in which the component elements find their logical validity. Interrelated in a conceptual framework, the various aspects interpenetrate each other to constitute a complex categorical scheme. Every consistent system becomes self-complete and self-contained in this way, apart from possible illogical departures from its starting point.

The truth of the Christian system is nonetheless in important respects evident even to the outsider. This awareness is due to the *imago Dei*, which, although sullied, survives universally in fallen humanity. Because of the presence of the *imago Dei* in the human species, no two persons have globally divergent sets of beliefs. In other words, the Christian worldview involves not merely an optional theoretical exposition of the totality of things, but also a universally shared prescientific understanding of reality, an understanding that includes a cognitive awareness of God, of other selves, and of the world as an intellectually correlated unity. Although some content of this belief system is always shared with another, that does not mean that all belief systems contain identical components of truth. The overarching interpretive framework in which beliefs are held lends decisive meaning to all particular components.

What invalidates secular views is their inability to account consistently for existence and meaning. Darwinism, for example, considers the rules of logic an evolutionary byproduct and thus views truth as changing. But in that event Darwinism cannot support the permanent validity of its own claims. Naturalism declares the universe to be a closed system of reality, but is colossally inconsistent when it affirms that human beings can creatively insinuate their preferred values into nature and history. Humanism insists that personality has no ultimate status in the universe, but is logically inconsistent when it affirms an ethically imperative social agenda congruent with universal human rights and dignity. Behaviorism insists that all human thought and conduct are matters of psycho-chemical determination; to present its views as transcendentally explanatory is clearly illogical. Existentialism affirms that personal commitment authenticates man as a value-creating agent; if that is so, it cannot then claim transcendent significance for ethical distinctions or affirm an objectively existing universe. However personally satisfying it may be, any worldview that requires resignation to a conceptual system plagued by logical inconsistency is unworthy of one's soul.

All systems other than the Judeo-Christian revelation are but partial or segmented; geometry is not botany, physics is not history. Only the Christian revelation embraces all of reality and can claim for its positions both validity and truth. Christians dispute the view that there is no ready-made realm of epistemic truth to which all human beings are related. They disown the theory that primal experience is unstructured and unmeaningful and that no basis exists for objective validity and truth. They reject pluralistic relativism that dismisses all religious frameworks as simply personal impositions on experience or privately preferred ways of structuring reality.

By the use of axioms and theorems, the Holy Spirit prods and persuades the mind to understand the nature of things and bends the will to believe the propositions that divine agency has enabled us to understand. The Christian worldview involves not simply theoretical axioms and postulated principles—that is, a preferred convictional complex that shapes one's outlook on reality and life. Instead, it offers truths foundational to all meaningful claims about existence and destiny. Alternative approaches predicated on a false starting point cannot rationally justify their claims.

Recent dialectical theology has boldly disavowed divinely revealed doctrinal truths. Even in certain Reformed circles some scholars now speak of revealed doctrines with great diffidence and even combine authentic Christian commitment with erroneous beliefs. Nicholas Wolterstorff, for example, remarks that "One might insist that . . . certain propositions . . . belong to the belief-content of all authentic Christian commitment. . . . Probably so, but certainly they will be few and simple."[53] In a footnote he adds: "It may even be that the belief-content of my authentic Christian commitment contains certain falsehoods. Frequently, in teaching children, one tells them what is, strictly speaking, false. So also it may be that some of what God says to us is, strictly speaking, accommodated to our frailty. Yet it may be that we are obliged to believe it."[54] Surely to suggest that divine revelation may convey falsehoods that we are obliged to believe and that authentic faith can rest on untruth is totally at variance with orthodox Biblical theism.

According to Max L. Stackhouse, some who are skeptical of reason now even "relativize reason by suggesting that the logics of Asia or Africa, or wherever, are entirely different from our masculine Western logic. . . .

Some believe this so deeply that they simply block out any evidence to the contrary—including the rather well-documented view that the denial of universal reason was one of the most important groundings of Fascism."[55] One might hope that in religion, as elsewhere, the flight from logic would be deplored rather than emulated.

The question remains whether comprehensively explanatory axioms and the deductions made from them would in fact constitute a metaphysics of reality or be merely a system of formal logic. Could a logically consistent system of propositions deduced from God as its point of departure disclose the fundamental structure of reality?

The objection to correlating logic and metaphysical reality now often stems from the assumption that the basic ontological structure of the universe is in evolutionary change. But such theory makes shipwreck of logic and reduces to nonsense any fixed and final assertion that can be made intelligibly about anything.

Thomas Aquinas held that God is first in ontological but not in epistemological order and that the existence of God cannot constitute the starting point for a process of deductive reasoning. But his attempt to argue from the not-God to the existence of God on the basis, moreover, of empirical observation and analogical method obscured the very metaphysical reality he hoped to champion.

Others have argued that to begin with God's existence and to deduce the reality of the world from God implies that divine Creation is a necessary principle; in that case, the world would issue pantheistically from God just as a conclusion issues from its premises. Metaphysicians therefore must not start with the existence of God, say these critics, if we are to avoid Spinoza's identification of the order and connection of things with the order and connection of ideas.

These objections are hardly convincing. To argue that there is no way to get from logical to metaphysical structure except on the basis of a pantheistic or idealistic epistemology is unpersuasive. If God is sovereign, any universe that derives from Him need not be anything other than voluntarily created. Indeed, some sort of irresistible emanation of a universe would denigrate the intrinsic divinity of God. Unless we are talking about a universe whose substance is nonmental, there is no reason why a logical system may not also at the same time constitute and express the very nature of reality. In a universe where the *Logos* is the source and support of created existence, logic is the *form* of reality.

FOUR

Drinking from Eternal Springs

Seldom in recent decades have Christian apologists put their best thought forward. The case for Biblical theism has often been stated in ways that appeal readily to popular but uncritical audiences, while disciplined scholars remain unpersuaded.

Ordinary believers—the kind who would have been much at home in the earliest Christian churches—are confident that Christianity has superlative credentials, even if they themselves may not be able to articulate them well. They can perhaps be forgiven if, in seeking intellectual vindication of evangelical orthodoxy, they hurriedly welcome presuppositions that promise a ready victory for their personal world and life commitments.

Some are encouraged, unfortunately, to think that they need "only believe"—not simply that God can veritably do what humans cannot, but also that to seek rational justification for the Christian hope is wicked. The fact is that "only believe" is a maxim that non-Christian religionists also can invoke. Such an appeal leaves one without warrants for choosing between many options.

Others are encouraged, equally unfortunately, to rely on unsound arguments for God's existence. Such arguments often involve logical leaps that exempt one from strenuous critical analysis. Evangelical spokesmen who venture to "prove" God from the universe, for example, seldom are found in the professional societies whose members are waiting to be convinced. Instead, religious popularizers commute among audiences eager to reinforce their faith by mere possibilities or probabilities rather than by logical validity.

Much confusion exists among those who eagerly point to experience in order to validate their beliefs. Only the least disciplined in philosophy would, to be sure, claim that the Christian faith is empirically or experientially *derived*. The God of the Bible is not perceptible to the senses, and a strictly empirical method has no competency to decide the reality of the supernatural. Some would insist that the Christian faith is empirically *verifiable*, either directly through the experience of the new birth or at least partially through an experiential confirmation of Biblical claims. But subjective experience cannot deal decisively with what transcends experience, and its conclusions in any event are tentative and revisable. Moreover, one's private personal experience, no matter how intense, cannot be made the ground of another person's religious affirmation, else we would face a host of competing claims unserviceable for distinguishing between true and false religion. If we profess to be Christian, neither our own experience nor anyone else's can be the basis of our religious affirmations.

More perturbing is the view that since Christian faith has core beliefs that are neither derivable nor verifiable empirically, we ought not present such beliefs to others unless we first render them credible on the ground of a non-revelational epistemology. In short, we are told, the case for theism is not to be presented on its own merits by affirming God-in-His-revelation as the basis of experience but is to be legitimated rather by an appeal to the not-God. This approach, as I see it, needlessly postpones the appeal to God-in-His-revelation, forfeits an inspired Scripture as its verifying principle, and lacks logical validity.

The issue here at stake involves a choice between so-called fideists, evidentialists, and rational presuppositionalists. In many fundamentalist churches and evangelical academic institutions, an evidentialist view prevails that is remarkably naive in respect to hidden presuppositions about "facts" and "proof." By leaping over any sustained discussion of its own covert assumptions, such evidentialism renders obscure any wide consensus on just what the evidence is supposed to "prove." Worse yet, some evidentialists claim the support even of the Protestant Reformers for a species of Thomistic scholasticism, as if Luther and Calvin were addicted to natural theology and to natural law. The Reformers, it is implied, taught that despite the Adamic Fall there survives universally in the human species a shared body of doctrinal truths and moral principles known independently of revelation. But if anything should be clear from a reading of the Reformers, it is surely that they were not Thomists, either wittingly or unwittingly.

Calvin contends that, despite the damage wrought by sin, human beings everywhere already believe in the existence of God whom we ought all to worship and obey. Were it not for sin, he taught, all humans would naturally believe in Him. "God himself," he writes, "has implanted in all men a certain understanding of his divine majesty" (*Institutes*, I, iii, 1). "Some conception of God is ever alive in all men's minds" (III, ix, 3). Calvin writes of sparks of light that even now universally brighten humanity. Fallen mankind is not without "some notions" of justice and rectitude and an awareness of God's glory and majesty and even of His omnipotence and justice. But Calvin nowhere converts this awareness into a universally shared body of doctrine that fallen humanity supposedly holds independently of divine revelation and on the basis merely of inference from empirical observation.

The question is sometimes asked why, if all persons know that God exists, we should go to all the trouble of seeking to vindicate the rational credibility of that belief. But theism is challenged by many rationalizations that need to be exposed for what they are. The so-called reasons for unbelief turn out routinely to be excuses that merely express rebellious desires.

At the other extreme a few influential fideists (who hold that no rational test whatever is appropriate to divine revelation) have needlessly promoted a misleading impression that all presuppositionalists are subjectivistic, dangerously irrational, and wholly unrelated to real life. They have encouraged the misunderstanding that evangelical presuppositionalism is arbitrary—that it disowns and demeans rationality and even defies reason.

An inevitable consequence of such extreme views, whether evidentialist or fideist, is an improper understanding of the relationship between presuppositions, faith, reason, and "facts." The ultimate outcome can only be a defective form of Christian belief and practice.

Among the weaknesses of much evangelical learning today is a neglect of primary sources that have helped to shape the history of thought. Consequently there is widespread unfamiliarity with the great debate over the relationship of revelation and reason.

During the successive centuries of Christian thought, revelation and reason have been portrayed in three strikingly different relationships: the Tertullian way, the Augustinian way, and the Thomistic way.[1] These contrasting descriptives divergently characterize revelation-and-reason relationships in terms of antithesis and synthesis.

The so-called Tertullian view (based on some of Tertullian's comments) excludes rational tests as inappropriate to revelation; indeed, revelation, it is said, confronts human reason as an absurdity or paradox and must be accepted solely on its own intrinsic ground. According to this fideistic approach, to seek in any way to justify revelatory faith on the basis of reason is to misconceive its nature; divine revelation calls for sheer faith in what necessarily confronts human reason as a paradox. Christianity requires belief, so fideists claim, in what confronts the unregenerate mind as essentially absurd. In the fideist view, divine revelation cannot and must not be rationally tested for validity and truth. No preliminary validation is proper that admits or allows revelation only on rational or logical grounds.

The primary link of Barth to fideism lies in his early insistence that divine revelation is nonpropositional, a premise that erodes the universal validity of revelation's content. Barth rejects all philosophical worldviews as intellectual barbarism and alien to the Word of God. His denial

that revelation contains valid truths, like his claim that the
Word of God is known only in inner decision and obedience, forfeits the intelligibility of divine disclosure and any
universal criterion of theological meaning and truth. Barth
held that divine revelation is not properly judged by finite,
sinful reason but transcends human categories of thought
and experience; its corollary, moreover, is faith, defined as
a divine gift of obedient response that does not involve
intellectual assent to propositions. But Christ and the apostles did not introduce novel techniques of understanding or
new tests of truth. They expected human beings to apply the
logical laws that are universally requisite to meaningful
thought.[2]

In contrast to fideism, the Augustinian and the
Thomistic views reject any exposition of revelation and reason in wholly antithetical terms. They insist that divine transcendent revelation is rational and that Christianity is
intellectually cohesive. Yet Augustine and Thomas differed
over whether Christian epistemology would begin with rev-
elation/faith or with empirical observation.

The Augustinian way was the way pursued not only
by Augustine, but also broadly by Anselm and the
Protestant Reformers. To be sure, Anselm sought to demonstrate the necessity for divine Incarnation and Atonement
without invoking Biblical revelation, and Luther claimed to
be a nominalist in philosophy despite his Augustinianism.
But they nonetheless broadly shared the conviction that rev-
elation/faith tends to rational understanding.

While, therefore, the Augustinian way begins with
faith, as does the Tertullian, it nonetheless diverges insis-

tently from fideism. Since the term *presuppositionalist* is now often loosely applied to anyone who begins with faith/revelation, rational presuppositionalists are easily confused with fideists who disallow any rational test of doctrinal beliefs. But the Augustinian way insists on intellectual warrants.

Rational presuppositionalism differs from fideism in that the former welcomes while the latter rejects the application to revelation of any tests of rational consistency and validity. It parts company with the emphasis often attributed to Tertullian—not always fairly[3]—that divine revelation confronts human reason as paradoxical. It strenuously resists the view of present-century dialectical and existential theologians that a necessary antithesis exists between revelation truth and metaphysical knowledge and that considers theology and philosophy as implacable foes.

Rational presuppositionalism, in contrast to fideism, does not sponsor a disjunction of faith and reason. It insists that all humanity can comprehend God's revelation and, moreover, can comprehend it prior to regeneration or special illumination by the Holy Spirit. Mankind in its present condition is capable of intellectually analyzing rational evidence for the truth value of assertions about God.

Over against the Thomistic espousal of natural theology, both Augustinian rational presuppositionalism and Tertullian fideism insist that divine revelation is the only way to know transcendent religious reality. The Thomistic way, by contrast, is evidentialist. It affirms that speculative understanding should precede faith/revelation. Thomas Aquinas presumed, therefore, to give logical proofs or demonstrations of the existence of God and of the soul and its immortality simply on the basis of empirical observation from the universe and without any appeal to revelation.

Over against fideism, rational presuppositionalism joins evidentialism in insisting on the intrinsic rationality of God and of His created universe. Objection to the Thomistic way concerns neither its advocacy of a legitimate theological role for reason nor its insistence on intelligible divine revelation; in both these respects, rational presuppositionalism and Thomism stand opposed to fideism. Sharp differences arise, however, over the Thomist claim to derive a supposedly demonstrative proof of God's existence from empirical observation alone, without recourse to revelation.

Christian rational presuppositionalism does not assume that philosophical reasoning is the only reliable source of knowledge. The mind of man is not veiled divinity. Transcendent divine revelation, not human reasoning, is the source of truth; publicly shared reason is a divinely gifted instrument for recognizing truth. In contrast to empiricists, a truly Christian epistemologist will not consider sensation alone as the source of unchanging knowledge, but will regard the verdicts of empiricism as inadequate and unstable.

Human reason has no inherent capacity to create enduring significance. What we humans project always has unsure relations to reality. The decisive issue about the interrelation of revelation and reason is whether we derive the governing content of philosophical reasoning from transcendent revelation, or whether we elevate human reasoning as a supreme or secondary instrument of revelation and therefore view it as a final authority alongside of or in lieu of the Word of God. Christian theism resists the intrusion of conjectural principles into the constitutive meaning of revelational truth.

The Bible, to be sure, does not present us with a comprehensively elaborated epistemology. But its content nonetheless implies a theory of knowledge and even provides important struts for such a theory. It does not look upon reason, for example, as a late evolutionary emergent that may sooner or later involve new and alternative laws of logic. Scripture unapologetically declares the *Logos* central to the Godhead. Indeed, Scripture affirms that God is the source and ground of reason and truth and that the *imago Dei* in which He created and preserves humanity includes rational and moral capacities. The Bible exhorts us to present ourselves to God, calling this a reasonable service (Romans 12:1).

It is especially necessary to focus on the role of contrasting presuppositions in divergent belief systems. Presuppositions are nothing less than crucial for the way one relates his or her experience to reality.

Christianity does not differ from other belief systems in that it has distinctive assumptions; all belief systems do. A belief system without presuppositions is like a sprawling edifice with neither an architectural plan nor secure foundations.

There is good reason for healthy skepticism about presuppositions, since human beings indulge in so many of them. The fact of this evident contrariety in no way justifies the prejudice, however, that no assumptions are valid. Yet in this age of spiritual vagabondage, not only unbelievers, but even many professing Christians have been encumbered with presuppositions that diverge not only from one another's but also from those of Biblical writers. All the more important becomes the question of legitimating warrants. Meaningful presuppositions are not without logical obligation. It will not do simply to raise to preferred status whatever assumptions are congenial to one's own prejudices. If we profess to deal with more than subjective opinion and to espouse transcultural truth, then the legitimacy or illegitimacy of particular presuppositions is crucially important.

Some comment is needed about the plea now and then voiced in behalf of "non-Western ways of thinking." There is, to be sure, much Western thought that has no more validity than much Asian or African thought. In our space-and-media age, competing and conflicting points of view are globally dispersed.

Yet some ecumenists disparagingly label evangelical orthodoxy as "Western" while they promote Neo-orthodox theology or Marxist-oriented social philosophy as if these alternatives were free of geographical roots, presuming them to be universal in significance. Some Latin American liberation theologians, for example, have disparaged capitalism as "North American" while promoting socialism as if it were indigenous.

But the real complaint now often heard about Western thinking rises from an assumption that oriental and occidental minds somehow function with essentially different forms of reasoning. Western thought, we are told, is ideally logical, whereas Eastern thought is intuitive or at any rate not much concerned with logical antitheses.

Underlying this contrast, of course, are two very different views of reality. Hindus and some Buddhists hold that ultimate reality is a divine All and consider human beings finite manifestations of divinity. All contrasts are engulfed by the all-inclusive Infinite; the Brahma-all or the Buddha-all embraces everything that exists. So-called sin is but finitude or incompleteness. Since the finite is essentially part of the Whole, any adverse divine judgment on the part would involve a divine repudiation of elements of its own nature.

Christianity, by contrast, affirms God to be the transcendent Other, the Creator of a space-time universe that is ontologically not-God. Humanity, to be sure, bears the *imago Dei* by creation, but this relationship is very different from that of part to whole. Moreover, humanity bears even the divine image only in some respects, most notably rational and moral capacities and rulership of the cosmos under God. No less importantly, the human race, fallen into spiritual rebellion, is under divine wrath with no prospect of redemption and restoration apart from the unmerited grace of God promised and fulfilled in Jesus Christ, the one incarnate, divine Mediator.

These conflicting views of essential human nature are more fundamental than racial or cultural differences.

Yet not even the oriental outlook is reducible to a view of reality in terms of part-and-whole rather than of creature-and-Creator. The so-called Asian way of thinking differs even among Asians. There is in fact no perspective, oriental or occidental, that would not be assisted by a good course in logic, or that does not soon sacrifice universal validity if it neglects the law of contradiction. The laws of logic are not a speculative prejudice imposed at a given moment of history as a transient philosophical development. Neither do they involve a Western way of thinking, even if Aristotle may have stated them in an orderly way. The laws of valid inference are universal; they are elements of the *imago Dei*. In the Bible, reason has ontological significance. God is Himself truth and the source of truth. Biblical Christianity honors the *Logos* of God as the source of all meaning and considers the laws of thought an aspect of the *imago*.

Not even humanity's Fall into sin has annulled the law of contradiction. The noetic effect of sin is serious, for it hinders man's disposition to meditate on the proper content of human thinking. But it does not deform or destroy the components of logic and reason. Propositions that were universally true before the Fall and belong to God's propositional revelation remain so ongoingly despite the Fall.

The pluralistic approach to world religions now often champions the need to recast the gospel in other than "Western thought forms" and in non-Western "logics," as if logic were an Aristotelian invention. Such emphases often relativize Christian theology and replace it with non-Biblical philosophy under the guise of Christian mission.

The arbitrary philosophical assumptions of destructive higher criticism have repeatedly crumbled under the crushing weight of intellectually inconsistent and Scripturally unsupported claims. We need not hurriedly accept the presuppositions that so readily dispose skeptical critics to attribute the Biblical books to alien writers, to assign them post-prophetic or post-apostolic dates, and to trace their teaching to alien traditions. Time and again what was proclaimed to be an achievement of objective scholarship by partisans of naturalism has sooner or later been seen to be but a reflection of questionable epistemological premises. A writer's meaning can be readily subverted by arbitrary assumptions concerning the purpose of the narrative; an interpreter's presuppositions have often deflected the textual sense from the author's intention. Current assumptions about the historicity of understanding dissolve the objectivity of truth claims—except (we should suppose) that of the historicity of understanding! Yet if modern savants like Heidegger and Bultmann can, without divine revelation, attain comprehensively valid information of their own kind, no objection can, in principle, be mounted against prophets and apostles who relay a transcendent disclosure on the basis of a divine initiative. The dogma of the historicity of understanding not only is destructive of the normativity of any and all communication, but also is self-destructive.

The Christian belief system is more comprehensive than are alternatives that shrink and distort ultimate reality. But that is not the only important thing to be said about Christianity. No logically inconsistent claims can be valid. Since Christianity stands the test of rational consistency, its control beliefs are not disqualified by the negative test of cognitive inconsistency. Moreover, Christianity has already passed through the scientific revolution; non-Biblical faiths must yet do so.

Christian faith, moreover, is not without evidential confirmation. Evidentialists point hurriedly to the world and man as evidence for God. But rational presuppositionalism points instead to Scripture. While evidentialists seek to erect a case for the infinite on the basis of the finite and profess to derive God as a conclusion from nature, rational presuppositionalists derive the cosmos instead from God, as did the writer of the Genesis creation account. So did the Apostle Paul when he addressed the professional philosophers gathered on Mars Hill (Acts 17:24ff.). Even in that great passage of Romans 1:18, where Paul emphasizes that God's universal and ongoing revelation of His eternal power and Godhead through nature penetrates mankind's deepest selfhood, the apostle puts the affirmation in the context of divine initiative; "God has made it plain to them" (1:19) is his governing premise.

What then would invalidate divine creation? If inspired Scripture taught that God did not create the universe! Evidentialists may point to order or harmony in nature as incontrovertible evidence or "proof" that God exists. But surely the disorder of nature—and not only its order—might also be compatible with God's existence. The fact is that the reality or existence of nature is not at all decisive for the existence of God.

Given a presuppositional theology, a question inevitably arises over the role of apologetics in the theological encyclopedia. It can, of course, serve the functions of clarifying beliefs, of challenging other worldviews and religions, and of implementing evangelistic persuasion. But it makes no pretense of defending Christianity in terms of its subscription to or compatibility with alien points of view. Rational revelation is its own best defense; every attempt to buttress it by appeals to vulnerable empirical arguments, evidences, or proofs can only do it a disservice.

All truth is ultimately God's truth, and the human mind is a divinely gifted instrument for recognizing it. The Holy Spirit uses truth as a means of persuasion. But Christian faith involves more than intellectual assent; it is in fact a comprehensive body-soul commitment. Faith is God's gift. The Holy Spirit links the validity of Christian claims to regenerating power.

The Christian belief system, which the Christian knows to be grounded in divine revelation, is relevant to all of life. For unbelieving multitudes in our times, the recent modern defection from God known in His self-revelation has turned the whole of life into a shambles. Ours is the first society in modern history to have ventured to erect a civilization on godless foundations; it may well be the last.

A somewhat softened naturalism (routinely called "secular humanism") is losing its smile as it deteriorates to grim paganism. The notably few fixed principles on which humanism insisted were clearly at odds with a conceptual canopy under which all claims are considered culturally relative and are engulfed by temporality. The face-saving humanist insistence on universal human dignity and rights and on ecological priorities was an attempt to graft a moral agenda onto a metaphysics of impersonal ultimate processes and events in which only transitory significance attaches to any and all cognitive and ethical imperatives. Naturalism can provide no conclusive reason why radical self-interest should not be the high altar on which all principles can be advantageously sacrificed. Indeed, naturalism can give no reason for taking reason or even itself seriously.

Pagan though they were, even the classic ancient Greek philosophers still warn us through their extant writings that no stable society can be built apart from durable truth and good and that any eclipse of these realities robs human survival of meaning and worth. Their writings are not the last word, however. Echoing from Creation to Calvary to Consummation, God's eternal Word invites a parched humanity to the Well that never runs dry, to the Water of Life that alone truly and fully quenches the thirst of stricken pilgrims.

NOTES

CHAPTER ONE: *Living at the Bottom of a Well*

1. Allan Bloom, *The Closing of the American Mind: How Higher Education Has Failed Democracy and Impoverished the Souls of Today's Students* (New York: Simon and Schuster, 1987).
2. Eric Voegelin, *Israel and Revelation*, Volume 1 of *Order and History* (Baton Rouge, LA: Louisiana State University Press, 1956), p. 316.
3. G. R. Beasley-Murray, *Jesus and the Kingdom of God* (Grand Rapids: Eerdmans/Paternoster, 1986).
4. Russell Hittinger, "Psychedelia and American Religion," *The World & I*, August 1988, p. 588.
5. Cf. Paul Van Buren, *The Edges of Language: An Essay in the Logic of a Religion* (New York: Macmillan, 1972).
6. The deconstructionist impact is now evident in the sphere of literature also. The French cult of literary critics paced by Roland Barthes energetically promotes the view that the author of a poem or novel is merely an initiatory moment to be displaced by the reader's creative stance (S/Z, Paris, 1970). This development, as David L. Jeffrey notes, involves the "destruction" of the author, the obliteration of the actual text, and ultimately the liquidation of literature ("Caveat lector: Structuralism, Deconstructionism, and Ideology," *Christian Scholar's Review*, XVII:4 [June 1988], pp. 436-448, p. 437). Language becomes unhinged from meaning, its reduction to a "free play of signifiers" becoming the underpinning for, in Jeffrey's words, "a critical-movement *inherently* committed to destruction of transcendent or referential

valuation in literature—and so, effectually, to eradication of the accumulated enterprise of 2000 years of enquiry in Western hermeneutics" (*ibid.*, p. 443). Monologic rhetoric and ideology displace intelligible speech and shareable truth. Thus Jacques Derrida has become the controversial forerunner of a cadre of literary critics, including Jonathan Culler, Paul deMan, Michael Riffaterre, and Barbara Johnson.

A related movement known as deconstructivism has arisen among architects who reject classical form and symmetry. Herbert I. London notes that they deliberately design buildings "that appear fragmented and accidental"—leaning walls, sloping floors, even walls and floors that don't touch. "The building justifies the goal of the creator when it appears to be on the brink of collapse" ("Architectural Anarchy," *American Arts Quarterly*, Summer 1988, pp. 16f.).

CHAPTER TWO: *Presuppositions and Theological Method*

1. Richard H. Poplin, "Fideism," in *The Encyclopedia of Philosophy*, 8 volumes, ed. Paul Edwards (New York: Macmillan, 1967), Volume 3, p. 201.
2. Peter L. Berger, *The Heretical Imperative: Contemporary Possibilities of Religious Affirmation* (Garden City, NY: Doubleday/Anchor Press, 1979).
3. Frederick Suppe, ed., *The Structure of Scientific Theories* (East Lansing, MI: Michigan State University Press, 1977).
4. William A. Rottschaefer, "The New Interactionism Between Science and Religion," *Religious Studies Review*, Volume 14, Number 3 (July 1988), pp. 218-224.
5. Carl F. H. Henry, *God, Revelation, and Authority*, 6 volumes (Waco, TX: Word Books, 1976-1984.) Volume 1: *God Who Speaks and Shows: Preliminary Considerations*.

CHAPTER THREE: *The Axioms of Biblical Theism*

1. Stephen F. Barker, "Geometry," in *The Encyclopedia of Philosophy*, 8 volumes, ed. Paul Edwards (New York: Macmillan, 1967), Volume 3, pp. 285-290, p. 290.
2. Philip Kitcher, *The Nature of Mathematical Knowledge* (New York: Oxford University Press, 1983).
3. Joseph W. Dauben, "Mathematics as Empirical," *Science*, Volume 225, Number 4664 (24 August 1984), pp. 825ff. (review of Kitcher, *The Nature of Mathematical Knowledge*).
4. Gordon H. Clark, "Atheism," *The Trinity Review*, July/August 1983, pp. 1-4, p. 4.

Notes

5. Alvin Plantinga, "Advice to Christian Philosophers," *Faith and Philosophy*, Volume 1, Number 3 (July 1984), pp. 253-271, p. 260.
6. Plantinga, "Advice to Christian Philosophers," p. 260.
7. *Ibid.*, p. 261.
8. Huston Smith, *Beyond the Post-Modern Mind* (New York: Crossroad, 1982).
9. Avery Dulles, *Models of Revelation* (Garden City, NY: Doubleday, 1983), pp. 30ff.
10. Ian G. Barbour, *Myths, Models and Paradigms* (New York: Harper & Row, 1974), pp. 30ff.
11. Norman Malcolm, *Thought and Knowledge: Essays* (Ithaca, NY and London: Cornell University Press, 1977), p. 212.
12. Dulles, *Models of Revelation*, p. 14.
13. C. S. Lewis, *Mere Christianity* (New York: Macmillan, 1945), p. 33.
14. Reinhold Niebuhr, *Christianity and Power Politics* (Hamden, CT: Shoestring Press/Archon Books, 1969), p. 207.
15. Nicholas Wolterstorff, *Rationality in the Calvinian Tradition*, eds. Hendrik Hart, Johan Van der Hoeven, and Nicholas Wolterstorff (Lanham, MD: University Press of America, 1983), p. 67.
16. James Orr, *The Christian View of God and the World*, 8th edition (Edinburgh: Andrew Elliot, 1970; reprint, Grand Rapids, MI: Eerdmans).
17. Bertrand Russell, *The Problems of Philosophy* (New York: Oxford University Press, 1912), p. 17.
18. Ludwig Wittgenstein, *On Certainty*, eds. G. E. M. Anscombe and G. H. von Wright, trans. D. Paul and G. E. M. Anscombe (New York: Oxford University Press, 1969), par. 105.
19. Lesslie Newbigin, *Foolishness to the Greeks: The Gospel and Western Culture* (Grand Rapids, MI: Eerdmans, 1986), p. 71.
20. Stephen Toulmin, *The Return to Cosmology: Postmodern Science and the Theology of Nature* (Berkeley, CA: University of California Press, 1982), pp. 25ff.
21. Richard Morris, *Dismantling the Universe* (New York: Simon and Schuster, 1983), p. 203.
22. Niels Bohr, *Atomic Theory and the Description of Nature* (New York: Macmillan, 1934).
23. Toulmin, *The Return to Cosmology*, p. 132. Cf. Arthur Koestler, *The Sleepwalkers* (New York: Macmillan, 1959).
24. Morris, *Dismantling the Universe*, p. 206.
25. *Ibid.*, p. 207.
26. D. Elton Trueblood, *Philosophy of Religion* (New York: Harper and Brothers, 1957), pp. 74ff.
27. Edward John Carnell, *An Introduction to Christian Apologetics* (Grand Rapids, MI: Eerdmans, 1956), pp. 89ff.

28. David Wolfe, *Epistemology: The Justification of Belief* (Downers Grove, IL: InterVarsity Press, 1982), pp. 35ff.
29. Karl R. Popper, *Conjectures and Refutations: The Growth of Scientific Knowledge* (New York: Harper & Row, 1968), pp. 33ff.
30. Stephen T. Davis, *Logic and the Nature of God* (Grand Rapids, MI: Eerdmans, 1983).
31. John Warwick Montgomery, *Where Is History Going? A Christian Answer to Secular Philosophies of History* (Grand Rapids, MI: Zondervan, 1969), p. 177.
32. Wolfe, *Epistemology*, p. 68.
33. Robert C. Sproul, John H. Gerstner, and Arthur Lindsley, *Classical Apologetics: A Rational Defense of the Christian Faith and a Critique of Presuppositional Apologetics* (Grand Rapids, MI: Zondervan, 1984), pp. 72ff.
34. Quoted in Daniel J. Boorstin, *The Discoverers* (New York: Random House, 1983), pp. 471ff.
35. Owen Gingerich, "Let There Be Light: Modern Cosmogony and Biblical Creation," in *Is God a Creationist? The Religious Case Against Creation Science*, ed. R. M. Frye (New York: Scribner, 1983), p. 133.
36. Frederick Hoyle, "The Universe: Past and Present Reflections," *Engineering Science*, November 1981, pp. 8-12.
37. Gingerich, "Let There Be Light," pp. 132, 135.
38. *Ibid.*, p. 136.
39. Wolfe, *Epistemology*, p. 57.
40. *Ibid.*, p. 15.
41. Frederick Copleston, *Religion and the One: Philosophers East and West* (New York: Crossroad, 1982), p. 38.
42. Gordon H. Clark, *Thales to Dewey* (Boston: Houghton Mifflin, 1957).
43. Gordon H. Clark, *A Christian View of Men and Things* (Grand Rapids, MI: Eerdmans, 1952).
44. Dorothy Emmet, *The Nature of Metaphysical Reality* (New York: Macmillan, 1967).
45. Wolfe, *Epistemology*, pp. 53ff.
46. *Ibid.*, p. 55.
47. Jerry H. Gill, *On Knowing God: Directions for the Future of Theology* (Philadelphia: Westminster, 1981), p. 144.
48. Newbigin, *Foolishness to the Greeks*, p. 64.
49. *Ibid.*, p. 148.
50. Copleston, *Religion and the One*, p. 252.
51. *Ibid.*, p. 254.
52. *Ibid.*, p. 255.
53. Nicholas Wolterstorff, *Reason Within the Bounds of Religion* (Grand Rapids, MI: Eerdmans, 1976), p. 71.

54. *Ibid.*, p. 113, n. 38.
55. Max L. Stackhouse, "An Ecumenist's Plea for a Public Theology," *This World*, 8 (Spring/Summer 1984): 47-79, p. 75.

CHAPTER FOUR: *Drinking from Eternal Springs*

1. Carl F. H. Henry, "Theology and Philosophy," in Henry, *God, Revelation, and Authority*, 6 volumes (Waco, TX: Word, 1976-1984), Volume 1: *God Who Speaks and Shows: Preliminary Considerations*, pp. 181-201.
2. Carl F. H. Henry, "The Method and Criteria of Theology," in *ibid.*, pp. 213-244.
3 In replying to Marcion, Tertullian writes of the Crhristian doctrines as offensive to reason:

> For which is more unworth of God, which is more likely to raise a blush of shame, that God should be born, or that He should die? that He should bear the flesh, or the cross? be circumcised or be crucified? be cradled or be coffined? be laid in a manger, or in a tomb? . . . You will not be "wise" unless you become a "fool" to the world, by believing "the foolish things of God." . . . The Son of God was crucified; I am not ashamed of it. And the Son of God died; it is by all means to be believed, because it is absurd. And He was buried, and rose again; the fact is certain, because it is impossible.

(*De Came Christi*, 6.1, 4 (*Corpus Christianorum, Series Latina*, Turnhout, 1953ff., Vol. I, p. 800, lines 2-9, p. 881, lines 26-29).

Oskar Skarsaune notes that the quotation is often abbreviated to *credo quia absurdum* "causing the misunderstanding that Tertullian was an early rationalist. That he was not. His argument was quite rational. The unbelievableness of the Christian doctrine of the incarnation reveals that it has not been not thought through [double negative is intentional] and in other words must be true." (*Incarnation—Myth or Fact?*, translated from the Norwegian by Trygve R. Skarsten [St. Louis: Concordia, 1990], Chapter 1, n. 16)

INDEX

Index

Index